Anxiou

MW00931892

A Guide and Workbook for Teens and Young Adults to Navigate Mental Health in the Digital Age

Frankie A. Albury

DEDICATION

To all those who struggle with anxiety and to the loved ones who support them—may you find understanding, resilience, and hope within these pages.

COPYRIGHT

© 2024 Frankie A. Albury. All rights reserved.

This book cannot be duplicated, saved in a retrieval system, or transmitted in any way—mechanical, electronic, photocopying, recording, or otherwise—without the author's prior written consent, except for brief quotes from reviews and critical articles.

ACKNOWLEDGMENTS

The creation of "Anxious Generation" has been a journey of discovery and collaboration. I am deeply thankful to all those who have supported me throughout this process.

First and foremost, I would like to thank my family for their unwavering support and patience. Your encouragement has been invaluable.

I am also grateful to my colleagues and friends who offered their expertise, insights, and feedback. Your contributions have greatly enriched this work.

LEGAL NOTICE AND DISCLAIMER

This book's content is solely intended for general informative purposes. It is not meant to replace expert medical advice, diagnosis, or treatment, nor should it be regarded as such. When you doubt a medical problem, consult your doctor or another trained healthcare professional. Pay attention to medical advice from a professional or put off getting it because of something you've read in this book.

The content in this book is accurate, complete, and appropriate, but the author and publisher make no claims or guarantees about it. Any liability resulting from using this book, whether direct or indirect, is disclaimed by the author and publisher.

At the time of publication, every attempt has been made to guarantee that the information provided herein is correct and comprehensive. On the other hand, the publisher and author disclaim all liability for any mistakes, deletions, or modifications to the content.

YOUR SPECIAL BONUSES

Thank you for clicking this book! As a token of my appreciation, I am excited to offer you three exclusive bonuses to enhance your experience and provide additional value.

Your Bonuses Include:

1. **Coping Strategies for Anxiety**
2. **Sleep Improvement Workbook**
3. **Work-Life Balance Workbook**

You can find these valuable resources on the last pages of this book.

Make sure to follow the guidelines and scan the QR Code

I hope you find them helpful and insightful as you work towards improving various aspects of your life.

Enjoy your bonuses and thank you for your support!

TABLE OF CONTENT

INTRODUCTION

Lili and Caleb, my teenage children, are bright, curious, and full of potential like most kids their age. Yet, I can't help but notice the undercurrent of anxiety that seems to permeate their lives. Take Lili, for instance. She's always been the kind of kid who dives headfirst into everything, from school projects to sports. But recently, I've seen a shift. Her once bubbly enthusiasm has been replaced by a constant worry about grades, friendships, and her future. The pressure to succeed, to be perfect, is overwhelming her. And it's not just Lili. Her younger brother, Caleb, is feeling it too.

Caleb, who used to spend hours playing outside, has now retreated into the digital world, his face often illuminated by the glow of his smartphone. He spends hours scrolling through social media, comparing his life to the carefully curated images of his peers. The other day, he mentioned feeling like he was falling behind and not doing enough, even though he's just 14. It's as if there's an invisible race they both feel they need to win, and it's taking a toll on their mental health.

Like so many of their friends, I've noticed that they are growing up in a world that seems to demand more from them every day. School isn't just about learning anymore; it's about competing— competing for grades, attention, and a spot in the next big opportunity. Lili spends hours studying, not just because she enjoys it but because she's terrified of failing. I've seen her break down in tears over an A-minus, convinced it's the beginning of a downward spiral.

And then there's Caleb. He's an excellent student but also deeply invested in his social life—online and offline. The digital world, which offers him connection and entertainment, also brings a relentless wave of comparison and self-doubt. He checks his phone constantly, his mood often swinging with the likes and comments on his latest post. It's as if his sense of self-worth is tethered to a digital thread, one that's easily frayed by a single negative comment or a friend's seemingly perfect life.

As a parent, it's heartbreaking to watch. I remember a time when childhood was about exploring the world at your own pace, making mistakes, and learning from them. But for Lili and Caleb, and so many kids like them, childhood has become a high-stakes game where the rules constantly change, and the pressure never lets up.

I see the effects of this pressure in the way Lili and Caleb interact with the world around them. Lili is often too stressed to enjoy the things she used to love. Her joy in learning has been overshadowed by the fear of not being good enough. On the other hand, Caleb seems to be losing touch with the real world; his attention is drawn more to his phone screen than to the people and experiences right before him.

What worries me most is that this anxiety is not just a phase they'll grow out of. It's a pervasive issue, one that is affecting an entire generation of young people. I've talked to other parents going through the same thing with their children. We share stories of sleepless nights, not just for our kids, but for us, as we worry about what kind of future they're heading into.

It's not hard to see where this anxiety comes from. The world Lili and Caleb are growing up in is vastly different from the one I knew at their age. The demands placed on them are immense, not just from school and social expectations but from the ever-present influence of technology. Social media, which could have been a tool for connection, has instead become a source of stress and insecurity.

Lili tells me about the pressure she feels to maintain a certain image online, to keep up with the latest trends, and to measure up to the flawless lives her friends portray on Instagram. Caleb, too, feels this pressure. He sees his friends' posts and wonders why his life doesn't seem as exciting or perfect. It's a constant comparison game, where the rules are rigged against them because what they see online isn't real—it's a highlight reel, carefully edited to show only the best moments.

As I listen to them talk, I realize they are part of what many call the 'anxious generation.' They are growing up in a time when the pressure to succeed, to be perfect, and to always be "on" is more intense than ever before. And it's taking a toll, not just on their happiness, but on their mental health.

I've tried to help Lili and Caleb navigate these challenges, but I often feel lost. How do you tell your child it's okay to be imperfect in a world that values perfection above all else? How do you encourage them to disconnect from their screens and engage with the real world when digital feels more immediate and rewarding?

I wrestle with these questions daily and know I'm not alone. Parents everywhere are grappling with the same fears and concerns. We want our children to be happy, healthy, and resilient, but the world they are growing up in makes that increasingly difficult.

In talking to other parents, I've realized that Lili and Caleb's issues are not unique to them. They are symptoms of a larger problem affecting young people all over the world. The problem is rooted in the pressures of modern life, the overprotectiveness of well-meaning parents, and the pervasive influence of technology.

What's clear is that something needs to change. We can't continue down this path where our children grow up anxious and afraid, always striving for an unattainable ideal. They need space to breathe, to make mistakes, and to discover who they are outside of the pressures of school, social media, and societal expectations.

As a parent, it's my job to help Lili and Caleb find that space and encourage them to take risks, fail, and learn from those failures. But it's also up to all of us—parents, educators, and society—to create an environment where they can do that, where they can grow up feeling supported, not suffocated, by the expectations placed upon them.

Lili and Caleb are just two of the many young people navigating this challenging landscape. Their stories are not unique, but they are important. They highlight the pressures facing today's youth and the impact those pressures are having on their mental health. It's time we take a closer look at these issues and find ways to support the next generation so they can grow up surviving and thriving.

OVERVIEW OF ADOLESCENT AND YOUNG ADULT MENTAL HEALTH CRISIS

Critical developmental transitions mark the journey from adolescence to young adulthood, each shaping a person's identity, relationships, and place in the world. During this period, individuals must navigate a complex set of challenges that influence their mental health in profound ways. These stages, identified through clinical work, research, and the lived experiences of young people, reflect the multifaceted nature of growing up in the modern world.

Adolescence often involves a shift from family-centered relationships to a broader social network, where peer relationships become increasingly significant. This period is characterized by exploring the self within the context of intimate relationships, engaging with the wider world, and discovering a sense of agency. Young people begin to understand who they are at their core, the role of friends in their lives, and the importance of finding a vocation that resonates with their emerging purpose and values.

However, this critical stage of development is also a time when the seeds of anxiety and depression are often sown. While some factors contributing to these mental health challenges may be present before adolescence, they tend to intensify during this period. What might start as episodic bouts of anxiety or depression can, with earlier onset, become chronic, leading to recurring episodes and, in some cases, multiple mental health disorders. The consequences of prolonged mental illness at this stage can be severe, impacting not only the individual's psychological well-being but also their ability to function effectively in various aspects of life.

The modern era presents unique and formidable challenges for adolescents and young adults today. Emotional balance, self-regulation, and self-awareness—key mental health components—must be developed against an increasingly complex and demanding landscape. Among the most pressing challenges facing this generation is the pervasive influence of digital technology, which often leads to disproportionate screen time and reduced face-to-face interactions. The rise of social media has created a new, usually unhealthy, emotional landscape where young people are constantly exposed to the curated lives of others, leading to feelings of inadequacy and increased social anxiety.

Parental overprotectiveness, while well-intentioned, has also played a role in shaping the mental health crisis. By shielding children from failure and risk, parents may inadvertently stifle their development of resilience and self-efficacy, leaving them ill-prepared to cope with life's inevitable challenges. The educational system, with its heavy emphasis on academic performance and standardized testing, often prioritizes grades over cultivating deep personal relationships and emotional intelligence. This environment can create a sense of constant pressure and competition, contributing to the anxiety and stress experienced by many young people.

Compounding these issues is the uncertainty of the world young people are growing up in. Rapid technological advancements, economic volatility, and shifting social norms have created a tower of uncertainty that looms over this generation. The transition to adulthood is no longer a straightforward path, and the anxiety of navigating these uncharted waters can be overwhelming.

Recent research underscores the severity of the mental health crisis among adolescents and young adults. Studies have documented a sharp increase in the prevalence of mental health issues in this population. A particularly striking finding is the rise in reports of "major distress" among 13- to 24-year-olds, which has escalated from 11.3 percent to 27.7 percent in just a few years. This alarming trend suggests that the mental health challenges facing today's youth are not isolated incidents but part of a broader, systemic issue.

What we are witnessing is not just a series of individual struggles but a generational crisis. The mental health of adolescents and young adults is being shaped by a confluence of factors—technological, social, educational, and economic—that are fundamentally altering the way they experience the world. As these young people transition into adulthood, the unresolved issues of their youth will likely carry forward, affecting their ability to thrive in an increasingly complex and demanding society.

Addressing this crisis requires a nuanced understanding of the unique challenges faced by this generation and a commitment to fostering environments that support their mental and emotional well-being. This involves not only reevaluating the role of technology in their lives but also rethinking educational practices, parenting approaches, and societal expectations. By doing so, we can begin to mitigate the factors contributing to this mental health crisis and help create a future where young people can develop into healthy, resilient adults.

Impact of Social Media and Smartphones on Teens and Young Adults

When I think about the countless hours my kids spend glued to their screens, it's hard not to wonder what all this connectivity is doing to them. We all know smartphones and social media are powerful tools—essential even for navigating modern life—but they come with some serious trade-offs, especially for teenagers and young adults. It's not just about the time spent online; it's about what that time is doing to their minds, sense of self, and mental health.

Dr. Parminder Kaur, a child and adolescent psychiatrist at the Mayo Clinic, shares these concerns. She's seen firsthand how the digital world, which was supposed to bring us closer together, is pulling us apart, especially when it comes to young people. The constant connectivity has turned toxic in ways we're only beginning to understand.

Think about it: Smartphones are now a permanent fixture in the lives of teens and young adults. For them, these devices aren't just tools—they're extensions of their identities. When you were a teenager, maybe you had a diary, a place to vent your frustrations and dreams privately. Today's teens? They have Instagram, TikTok, and Snapchat, public platforms where they constantly perform and validate. Every like retweet, and follower count becomes a measure of their worth, a benchmark of their success in this digital age.

But here's the thing: The validation they get online is fleeting. It's a quick dopamine hit, a momentary high that leaves them wanting more. It's not real, and deep down, they know it. But the brain's reward system doesn't care. It's been hijacked by these digital stimuli, keeping them hooked and, in many cases, leading to a cycle of anxiety and stress that's hard to break. You've probably seen it yourself—how your kids or grandkids light up when their phone buzzes and panic when a post doesn't get enough likes.

We like to think of social media as a way to stay connected, but it's become a source of stress and comparison for many teens and young adults. They're constantly exposed to the highlight reels of others' lives—the perfect vacation photos, the flawless selfies, the curated images of success. It's easy to forget that these images are just that—curated. They don't show the struggles, the insecurities, the messy realities of life. But when you're young and impressionable, it's hard not to compare yourself to these idealized versions of reality and feel like you're falling short.

My daughter Lili once told me that she feels like she's living in two worlds: real and digital. In the real world, she goes to school, hangs out with friends, and tries to figure out who she is. The digital world is where she performs—she puts on a show for her followers, crafting an image of herself that she hopes others will like. But that performance is exhausting, and it's taking a toll on her mental health. She's not alone. Many of her friends feel the same way, caught in a web of expectations that no one can realistically meet.

Caleb, my son, is a little different. He's quieter and more introspective, but I also see the effects on him. He's not as obsessed with social media as Lili, but he's just as tied to his smartphone. It's his connection to the world, a lifeline that he can't seem to cut. But I worry about the nights he stays up late, scrolling through endless feeds, losing sleep over things that shouldn't matter. Sleep is crucial, especially for developing minds, yet many young people sacrifice it to stay connected.

And it's not just about sleep. The constant use of smartphones and social media is changing how young people interact with the world around them. Face-to-face conversations are being replaced by text messages and DMs. Superficial online connections are overshadowing deep, meaningful relationships. And while technology makes it easier than ever to stay in touch, it's also making it harder for young people to develop the social skills and emotional intelligence they need to navigate the complexities of life.

The mental health implications are profound. We're seeing an increase in anxiety, depression, and other mental health issues among teens and young adults, and much of it can be traced back to their digital lives. A recent survey found that the number of young people reporting "major distress" has nearly tripled in just a few years. This isn't a coincidence. It's a clear sign that the digital world, with all its benefits, is also a minefield for mental health.

But it's not just the mental toll we need to worry about. The impact on physical health is real, too. We're seeing more sedentary lifestyles, as young people spend hours on their devices instead of being active. The effects on their sleep, as I mentioned, are well-documented. But there's also the impact on their ability to focus and engage in deep, uninterrupted thought—crucial for learning and personal growth.

Focusing on anything for a long time is hard when constantly distracted by notifications.

As parents, educators, and society, we must recognize these challenges and find ways to address them. It's not about demonizing technology—after all, it's here to stay—but about finding a balance. We need to teach our young people how to use these tools in a way that enhances their lives rather than detracts from them. We need to help them build resilience, understand that likes or followers don't measure their worth, and encourage them to disconnect sometimes to engage with the world around them in meaningful ways.

It's a daunting task, but it's also an essential one. Because if we don't, we risk losing a generation to the pressures and pitfalls of the digital world. And that's something none of us want to see.

CHAPTER ONE
THE DECLINE OF PLAY-BASED CHILDHOOD

"When play is replaced by schedules and screens, we lose not just the laughter of children, but the creativity and resilience that free play fosters."

One of the most troubling changes in the lives of today's youth is the dramatic reduction in their time for free, unstructured play. Play, in its purest form, has always been the quickest route to joy and satisfaction. For generations, kids instinctively knew how to fill those precious free hours—running outside, inventing games, building forts, or simply letting their imaginations run wild. This wasn't just about entertainment; it was about learning how to navigate life and developing the creativity, resilience, and problem-solving skills crucial for becoming independent.

In those early years, a child's mind is like a fresh canvas, ready to be filled with the colors of experience and discovery. Play is their brush, crafting their understanding of the world through trial and error, exploration, and sheer delight. When kids are left to their own devices—without schedules, rules, or adult interference—they engage in play essential for their development. During these moments, their minds, bodies, and personalities are in their most vibrant, thriving state.

But what happens when that time for play is taken away? Why can't today's young people relax, connect with others, and enjoy being kids? The answer is often dismissed with a wave of the hand: "It's just the pressures and worries of growing up. That's just how it is now." But something about that explanation feels deeply wrong.

It's easy to point fingers—at society, the education system, the government, the media, other adults, or even the parents themselves. We all like to say that children are our most valuable resource and that they are our future. Yet, we seem to be failing to protect that very resource. We're not giving them the space to breathe, unwind, or just be. Instead, we're filling their lives with structured activities, academic pressures, and a constant push to achieve, leaving little room for the unstructured play vital to their well-being.

The reduction of playtime is not just a loss of fun—it's a loss of something much deeper. Play is not a frivolous activity; it is the work of childhood. Through play, children experiment with the roles they will later take on in life, and they learn how to manage risk, cooperate with others, and handle emotions. Play is where they discover who they are and what they are capable of. When we take that away, we're not just taking away their joy but their ability to grow into well-rounded, confident adults.

The consequences of this shift are far-reaching. With enough free play time, children can experience essential developmental opportunities. They are less likely to develop the independence and resilience they need to face life's challenges. They're also more likely to experience stress and anxiety, as they're constantly being told—implicitly or explicitly—that what matters most is their ability to perform, to achieve, to succeed. And when every moment is scheduled, when every activity is monitored, where is the time for them to just be themselves?

We must ask ourselves, what kind of adults do we want our children to become? If we continue on this path, we risk raising a generation that knows how to excel in school, how to meet expectations, and how to navigate a highly structured world—but not necessarily how to think creatively, how to take risks, or how to find joy in the simple, unstructured moments of life.

It's time to reconsider what we value in childhood. We must recognize that play is not a luxury but a necessity. It's how children prepare for life, learn the skills that no classroom can teach, and build the foundations for a healthy, balanced adulthood. By giving them back their time to play, we're not just giving them a chance to have fun—we're allowing them to grow into the kind of people who can lead us into the future.

Let's stop saying that "this is just how it is" and ask how we can improve. Let's value our children for who they are now, not just for who they might become. And let's give them the space they need to play, explore, and discover the world on their terms. Only then can we truly prepare them for the challenges of tomorrow?

HISTORICAL CONTEXT OF CHILDHOOD DEVELOPMENT

By the 19th century, society began to reassess the treatment and status of children fundamentally. Before this period, children were often seen as small, powerless beings with no rights or voice. They were expected to be miniature adults, working in harsh conditions or being groomed to fit societal norms without much consideration for their individuality or emotional well-being. Influential figures like Charles Dickens and Inspector Thomas Barnardo became vocal advocates for the better treatment of children, highlighting their suffering and advocating for change. Their efforts were instrumental in bringing about a shift in how children were perceived and treated.

As psychology began to emerge as a distinct field during this time, there was a growing interest in understanding the mental health of young people. This led to a greater recognition of childhood as a unique and important stage of life, deserving of protection and care. Alongside this came the push for children's rights and the restriction of child labor, as society slowly began to acknowledge that children were not just blank slates to be molded but individuals with their own needs and potential.

In 1877, the notion of a moral obligation to ensure the emotional well-being of children started to gain traction. Despite this, children were still largely seen as "blank slates" upon which educators and parents could write their aspirations and goals. The idea that parental responsibility extended beyond just providing physical care began to take root, leading to the first adoption agency regulations in 1912, emphasizing the importance of family involvement in a child's upbringing. Even then, adults were seen as the primary architects of a child's future, and one of the leading child guidance clinics of the time reported that 80 percent of its cases involved active parental participation.

However, despite these advancements, the emphasis remained on preparing children for their future adult roles rather than on their current emotional or psychological needs. Throughout the 17th and 18th centuries, children were often ignored unless they exhibited adult-like behavior. In the art of the time, children were portrayed primarily as symbols of wealth and status rather than as individuals in their own right. It wasn't until the 19th century that we began to see decorative items and portraits depicting children as carefree and contented beings, reflecting a slowly growing appreciation for the innocence and distinctiveness of childhood.

Yet, even with these changes, the primary focus remained on grooming children to meet societal expectations. Physical well-being and proper education were prioritized as means of exerting control and normalization over young minds. Children were expected to conform to the "fashionable new puppet" stage of life, where their value was judged based on how well they could adhere to moral and social standards. The idea of nurturing their emotional well-being or considering the complexities of their experiences was still far from the norm.

In essence, while the 19th century marked significant strides toward recognizing the importance of childhood, it was still a time when adults were the gatekeepers of a child's development. The understanding that children have their own emotional and psychological needs, separate from the expectations placed upon them, was only beginning to emerge. As society continued to evolve, the seeds planted during this era would eventually grow into the more comprehensive and compassionate approaches to childhood development that we strive for today.

CULTURAL SHIFTS IN PARENTING AND SOCIETAL EXPECTATIONS

You've probably noticed how different things are for you compared to when your parents were your age. It feels like the world expects a lot from you, right? Whether it's your grades, your plans, or even how you handle your emotions, it seems like there's always something that you need to be working on. But this isn't just about you—how parenting and society's expectations have shifted over the years.

Think about it: your grandparents or parents grew up when kids were often left to figure things out independently. They had much more freedom to explore, make mistakes, and be kids. But somewhere along the way, things changed. Every moment of your life is monitored, every decision weighed, and every failure dissected.

It's not that your parents don't want you to have fun or enjoy being a teenager—they do. But they're also dealing with a lot of pressure themselves. Society has shifted in a way that now emphasizes raising you to be a good person and ensuring you're mentally and emotionally prepared for the future. Your parents are expected to be involved in every aspect of your life, from schoolwork to social life to emotional well-being.

And let's be honest, sometimes it feels too involved, right? Like they're always hovering, ensuring you don't mess up. That's where terms like "helicopter parenting" and "snowplow parenting" come from—parents who are always there, trying to clear the way for you so you don't have to face too many challenges. But, while they're doing this out of love and concern, it can sometimes feel like they're not letting you breathe.

You might hear older generations talk about how your generation is more anxious and stressed. They look at how your parents are always around and think, "No wonder these kids are so anxious—they never get a break from their parents!" And there's some truth to that. When you're always being watched, it's hard to feel like you can just be yourself, make mistakes, and learn from them.

But it's not just about your parents—about the world they're raising you in. Your parents are dealing with a constantly changing society, with new challenges that didn't exist when they were your age. The job market is tougher, the cost of living is higher, and the pressure to succeed is everywhere. So, they feel like they have to be more involved and protective because the stakes seem so much higher now.

And then there's the impact of social media. You know how it is—every time you post something, there's that little hit of excitement when you get likes or comments. But there's also the stress of trying to keep up with everyone else, of feeling like you always have to be "on." Your parents see that, too, and worry about how it affects you. So, they step in even more, trying to guide you through a world different from the one they knew growing up.

It's easy to feel frustrated with them, like they're being too controlling or worried about things that don't seem like a big deal to you. But remember, they do it because they care, even if it doesn't always feel that way. They're trying to navigate this strange new world of parenting just as much as you're trying to figure out how to grow up in it.

But here's the flip side: all this involvement and pressure can make developing the independence you need hard. You need space to make your own decisions, to mess up, and to figure out how to fix things on your own. That's how you build confidence, how you learn to trust yourself. And deep down, your parents know this too. They must find the balance between being there for you and letting you grow independently.

So, the next time you feel like your parents are breathing down your neck, try to see it from their perspective. They're just as stressed and anxious about getting it right as you are. Maybe it's time for a real conversation about how you can work together to give you the space you need while knowing they've got your back when required. After all, growing up isn't just about learning to do things independently—it's also about learning to understand each other, parents and teenagers alike.

Chapter Note

CHAPTER TWO
THE RISE OF PHONE-BASED CHILDHOOD

"As digital devices redefine childhood, we must examine how this transformation shapes young minds."

- Sherry Turkle

I remember when chatting with friends meant something different. Back then, it was a special privilege, not an ever-present lifeline. Today, for kids, it's like an extra limb—always there, always within reach. This constant connection, though, has brought with it some unexpected changes, especially when it comes to how they interact with the world around them.

Growing up, I was part of the last generation that still knew life without a smartphone. We didn't have the luxury of instant communication; we had to make plans, meet up in person, and figure things out on our own. Sure, we had landlines, but it wasn't the same. There was a kind of freedom in not being tethered to a device, in not having a virtual friend in your pocket 24/7.

But that's not the world kids are growing up in today. For them, the smartphone isn't just a tool; it's a lifeline. It's how they stay connected, how they interact, and, increasingly, how they form their sense of self. Unlike the baby boomers, who spent their youth outdoors, playing with neighborhood friends, today's kids are more internally focused. They're growing up in a world where trips to town or meeting up with local peers isn't always an option because they rely on their parents for transportation. And with both parents often working long hours, those spontaneous, in-person interactions have become rare.

Instead, kids are more likely to be linked to each other through screens. But here's the thing: while they're constantly connected, they're also missing out on something crucial—those real-life social cues that help build genuine friendships. These are the kinds of lessons you learn on the playground, in face-to-face conversations, where you can see a smile, hear a laugh, or feel the sting of a disagreement. But when your interactions are mostly virtual, those lessons come at a different pace, if they come at all.

I've seen it with my own kids. The things that used to come naturally—like picking up on social cues or learning how to navigate conflicts with friends—are now harder for them. It's not that they're lacking in social skills, but the skills they're developing are different. They're growing up in a world where you can disconnect with a swipe, where "friends" are people you've never met in person, and where the messiness of real relationships can be avoided by simply logging off.

This shift has its consequences. We're seeing a rise in anxiety among young people, and it's not hard to see the connection. When your social life is mediated by a screen, it's easy to misunderstand or misinterpret what's happening. A joke might not land the same way in a text as it would in person. A lack of likes on a post can feel like a personal rejection. And when your primary interactions are online, you miss out on the chance to learn and grow from the small mistakes and missteps that are a natural part of childhood.

What's more, the dynamic between generations has changed. When I was a kid, there were those moments when you wanted to assert your independence, those "God, Mum!" moments where you tried to prove you could handle things on your own. But for today's kids, those moments are different. With a virtual friend always available, there's less need to push for independence. They can retreat into their screens, avoiding the messiness of real-world relationships until they're much older.

As we look at the increase in anxiety among young people, it's clear that the rise of phone-based childhood plays a significant role. Today's kids are growing up in a world where constant communication is the norm, but it's a different kind of communication. It's filtered through screens, stripped of the nuance that comes with face-to-face interactions. And while this connectivity can offer a sense of security, it also creates new pressures and anxieties.

It's easy to romanticize the past, to think that things were simpler and better before smartphones took over our lives. But the reality is more complex. The world has changed, and so have the challenges that kids face. The key is finding a balance—helping them navigate this digital landscape while also ensuring they don't lose touch with the real, messy, beautiful world around them.

So, as parents, educators, and members of the community, we need to be aware of how these shifts are affecting our kids. We need to help them develop the skills they need to thrive, both online and offline. And we need to make sure they don't miss out on the joy and connection that comes from real, in-person relationships. Because no matter how advanced our technology becomes, there's still nothing quite like the experience of playing outside with friends, of learning how to navigate the ups and downs of real-life friendships, and of growing up in a world that values human connection over digital convenience.

INTRODUCTION OF SMARTPHONES

We live in a time of incredible technological advances, yet, ironically, many of us struggle to embrace and enjoy this modern life fully. For instance, smartphones have revolutionized how we connect, work, and navigate our lives. But alongside these benefits, there's a darker side that's increasingly difficult to ignore. In the fast-paced world of business, fear has become a constant companion. The anxiety of being sidelined, downsized, or left behind by the relentless march of technology is pervasive, and smartphones are both a symptom and a cause of this unease.

Anxiety is different from stress—it's deeper and more insidious. When you're anxious, your body kicks into high gear, flooding your system with cortisol and preparing you for a fight-or-flight response as if facing an immediate physical threat. But in today's world, the threats aren't tangible—they're deadlines, notifications, and the fear of missing out. Your body, however, doesn't know the difference. It shuts down non-essential functions like digestion and growth, focusing all its energy on dealing with this perceived danger. This constant state of alertness can quickly become overwhelming, leaving you feeling lost and adrift in a sea of obligations and expectations.

Smartphones, in particular, have transformed how we interact with the world, but they've also heightened our awareness of every stressor and potential threat. Every buzz, ping, or alert pulls us further into a cycle of anxiety, constantly reminding us of what we haven't done, what we might be missing, or what we should be worrying about next. It's as if we've traded peace of mind for permanent vigilance.

This isn't just a personal issue but a societal norm. Even those who seem the most put-together—leaders, professionals, and decision-makers—are grappling with unprecedented levels of anxiety. For those deeply connected to the digital world, particularly in the white-collar sector, the intensity of modern life can be overwhelming. The rapid pace of change, the constant flow of information, and the endless demands on our attention are taking a toll on our mental and physical health.

The 21st century has brought a unique kind of fatigue—not just physical tiredness but deeper exhaustion from our lives relentless newness, speed, and complexity. Stress has always been a part of the human experience, but the kind of stress we're dealing with now is different. It's a byproduct of a world that's always on, connected, and demanding more. While stress can sometimes drive us to achieve great things, pushing us to earn qualifications, tackle challenges, and break new ground, it can also be destructive, leading to burnout, anxiety, and a sense of being perpetually overwhelmed.

The introduction of smartphones has played a significant role in this shift. What was once a tool for connection and convenience has become a source of constant pressure. We're more connected than ever, yet we feel more isolated, anxious, and uncertain about our place in the world. It's a tragic irony that in our quest to stay ahead, we've created a reality where the tools designed to help us now contribute to our greatest challenges.

EARLY 2010S AND THE SHIFT IN CHILDHOOD DYNAMICS

For decades, there was a widespread belief among the educated elite that the digital age would usher in a new era of growth and opportunity for young people. The narrative was optimistic, filled with promises of a bright future where the so-called "Digital Natives" would thrive in a world tailored to their strengths. We were fed a steady diet of headlines and articles proclaiming the rise of "Digital Resiliency" and the advent of a generation that would effortlessly navigate the complexities of the modern world. Terms like "Citizens of the World" and "Millennials in an Age of Empowerment" painted a picture of a generation perfectly equipped to handle whatever came their way.

But as the early 2010s unfolded, it became increasingly clear that the reality for these young people was far more complicated—and far less rosy—than anyone had anticipated. The youngest members of the millennial generation, those born in the late 1990s and early 2000s, were entering their teenage years just as the world around them was undergoing rapid and unsettling changes. These teens were the first to experience constant digital access from a young age, making them pioneers in navigating the uncharted waters of social media, 24/7 connectivity, and an increasingly online existence.

At the same time, these young people were coming of age during a period marked by significant global upheaval. The early 2010s were a time of perpetual conflict, economic instability, and growing political and social tensions. For many of these teenagers, the promises of digital utopia clashed with the harsh realities of a world in turmoil. The gap between the optimistic narratives they were raised on and the reality they faced led to a growing sense of disillusionment.

This generation, often called the "gateway generation," bore the brunt of these contradictions. They were told they were the future, the ones who would inherit and fix the problems left behind by previous generations. But instead of inheriting a world of possibility, they found themselves amid a mental health crisis that no one had prepared them for. As they navigated the digital landscape, they also had to contend with the fallout from economic decline, rising inequality, and the erosion of traditional support systems.

Where once the diverse experiences of growing up might have brought excitement and a sense of opportunity, these young people were increasingly met with a sense of crisis. Public discourse and policy began to shift, focusing on the alarming rise in mental health issues among children and teenagers. Headlines about "a crisis in children's mental health" became all too common, as did reports of years-long waitlists for the few mental health professionals and programs available.

A wave of do-it-yourself (D.I.Y.) initiatives emerged in response to this growing crisis. Grassroots efforts, community-led projects, and peer support networks started to fill the gaps left by the failing system. Often frustrated by the lack of formal support, young people and their families turned to these alternative solutions to find the care and guidance they desperately needed.

The early 2010s marked a significant shift in childhood dynamics, defined by the clash between the glossy promises of the digital age and the grim realities of a world in crisis. The narratives of digital empowerment and global citizenship were no match for the challenges these young people faced. Instead of being the happiest generation, as some had optimistically proclaimed, they became the generation that struggled under unrealistic expectations and a system ill-equipped to support their needs.

SELF-REFLECTION QUESTIONS

In a comfortable and quiet space with minimal distractions, take 30 minutes to contemplate the following 18 questions. There are no right or wrong answers. The exercise aims to provide information for self-reflection to analyze the intensity and context of your relationship with digital devices, what factors might be influencing this, and to identify areas for moderation. Your responses will be anonymous. After you have completed the exercise, consider sharing the results of your self-reflection with others in your immediate circle whose relationship with digital devices might warrant some moderation.

1. How often do you check your smartphone or other digital devices throughout the day?

_____

_____

_____

2. Do you feel anxious or uneasy when you are without your digital devices (e.g., phone, tablet) for some time?

_____

_____

_____

3. How many hours daily do you actively use digital devices for non-work or non-school-related activities?

_____

_____

_____

4. Are there specific times or situations where you feel compelled to use digital devices even when you may not need to?

_____

_____

_____

_____

5. Do you mindlessly scroll through social media or digital content without a specific purpose?

_____

_____

_____

_____

6. How often do you use digital devices during meals, conversations, or other social interactions?

_____

_____

_____

_____

7. Have you noticed a change in your sleep patterns or quality due to digital device use?

_____

_____

_____

8. Do you experience physical symptoms such as eye strain, headaches, or neck pain related to prolonged use of digital devices?

_____

_____

_____

_____

9. Are there particular apps or websites you find difficult to stop using once you start? If yes! Why?

_____

_____

_____

_____

10. Have you ever felt overwhelmed or stressed by the amount of information or notifications you receive from digital devices?

_____

_____

_____

_____

11. Do you compare yourself to others based on what you see on social media or other digital platforms?

_____

_____

_____

12. How often do you engage in offline activities (e.g., hobbies, exercise, reading) compared to online activities?

_____

_____

13. Do you feel a sense of relief or relaxation when you disconnect from digital devices for some time?

_____

_____

_____

14. Are there times when you prioritize digital device use over other important tasks or responsibilities?

_____

_____

_____

15. Have you ever tried to reduce your digital device use, and if so, what challenges did you face?

_____

_____

_____

16. Do you use digital devices to cope with boredom, stress, or negative emotions?

_____

_____

_____

17. How does using digital devices impact your relationships with family, friends, or coworkers?

_____

_____

_____

_____

18. Reflecting on your answers, what changes would you like to make to your relationship with digital devices?

_____

_____

_____

_____

Chapter Note

CHAPTER THREE
THE MECHANISMS OF MENTAL HEALTH DECLINE

"We are more connected than ever before, yet we are witnessing an unprecedented rise in mental health issues among our youth. It is imperative to understand the underlying mechanisms driving this decline." -
Jean Twenge

We've all felt it at some point—the tightening in the chest, the racing thoughts, the worry that something could go wrong in a social situation. But what's happening now goes beyond those occasional bouts of social anxiety that everyone experiences. It's become clear that entire generations are grappling with a profound disconnection, not just from each other but from the very fabric of human interaction. It's as if the ability to engage in simple, face-to-face conversations is slipping away, replaced by a growing discomfort, even fear, of such encounters.

You might have noticed it in yourself or those around you: the hesitation to pick up the phone and call someone, the avoidance of spontaneous conversations, or the tendency to rely on text and social media instead of meeting in person. What's more troubling is how this discomfort also extends into the digital world. Many people feel paralyzed by the thought of engaging online, not just because of the usual worries about how they'll be perceived but because the very act of communication has become fraught with anxiety.

This rigidification of social interactions creates significant challenges, especially when understanding and connecting with others on a meaningful level. It's no longer just about avoiding awkwardness; it's about a fundamental breakdown in the ability to relate to one another. This is particularly evident in many's struggles to find common ground with others, especially across gender lines. The basic skills of conversation and empathy, which once formed the foundation of social relationships, are becoming harder to cultivate.

In this modern era of technological advancements and constant connectivity, the prevalence of social anxiety and interpersonal disconnect has reached new heights. It is disheartening to see how the tools designed to bring us closer together often pull us apart. As people become more engrossed in their virtual worlds, they lose sight of the value of authentic, face-to-face interactions. The impact of this disconnection is profound, leading to a generation grappling with isolation, social paralysis, and a deep sense of loneliness.

Consider the characters from Heinrich Hoffmann's famous 1845 children's book, such as Fidgety Phil, the Bearded Lady, or Mr. and Mrs. Grumpledump. These eccentric personalities navigated a world filled with peculiarities and challenges like today's generation. They represent the timeless struggles of fitting in and finding one's place in a society that often feels confusing and unforgiving. Today's young people face similar battles, not with mischievous characters in a storybook but with the complexities of a rapidly changing world.

This disconnection stretches far beyond personal relationships. Even basic conversations have become a source of distress for many. The fear of judgment and rejection is so pervasive that it casts a shadow over every interaction. People long for connection, yet they feel trapped by their insecurities, leading to a constant push and pull between the desire for social interaction and the fear of it. This contrast between what we want and experience is a hallmark of the modern social landscape, reflecting a deeper issue that needs to be addressed.

It's crucial to understand that while technology has undoubtedly revolutionized our lives, it has also introduced new forms of social anxiety and disconnection. The overwhelming accessibility to online platforms and digital communication has made people more socially fragile, fostering a fear of genuine human interaction. In many cases, what was supposed to make communication easier has done the opposite, creating barriers where there should be bridges.

As you look around, it becomes clear that losing face-to-face interactions and authentic dialogue is a significant challenge for today's society. The world has become where navigating social dynamics requires more effort, understanding, and grace than ever. The whimsical characters of Hoffmann's book remind us that these challenges are not new, but their modern manifestations are uniquely tied to the digital age we live in.

Social anxiety, defined as the overwhelming fear of negative judgment, criticism, or rejection in any social situation, is not just a passing discomfort. For those who experience it, this fear can be debilitating, seeping into every aspect of life. It's a psychological disorder that goes far beyond simple shyness. Recent studies have shown that approximately one-third of young adults exhibit symptoms of social anxiety—a staggering 25% increase compared to three and a half decades ago. This surge is partially attributed to the proliferation of Internet-based communications, which have become integral to our daily lives.

You might think these digital platforms would alleviate nervousness, offering a less intimidating environment for connection. But the reality is far different. Social networking sites, instead of easing anxiety, often amplify it, leading to even greater feelings of loneliness and isolation, especially among younger generations. The pressure to present a perfect image online and maintain a certain number of likes or followers can be overwhelming, creating a vicious cycle of anxiety and disconnection.

The impact of social anxiety extends far beyond the occasional awkward moment. It permeates relationships, work, and personal fulfillment, trapping individuals in a cycle of self-doubt and fear. Those who struggle with social anxiety often find themselves second-guessing their every action, word, and appearance, undermining their ability to form meaningful connections and stifling their personal growth. This acute self-consciousness leads to emotional isolation, making it difficult to engage fully with the world around them.

But the effects of social anxiety aren't confined to individuals. They ripple out, affecting society as a whole. When people are too afraid to participate in social settings, it hinders the free exchange of ideas, stifles creativity, and limits the potential for vibrant, diverse communities. Social anxiety is not just a personal issue; it's a societal challenge that requires collective understanding and action.

In conclusion, social anxiety represents a complex web of fears, anxieties, and self-doubt that can significantly impact a person's well-being. It's important to recognize the distinction between social anxiety and shyness, as well as to understand the role of technology in exacerbating these feelings. By fostering compassion and creating inclusive spaces, we can help those struggling with social anxiety break free from their limitations and build connections that enrich their lives. In doing so, we can work towards a society that values and supports genuine human interaction, even in the digital age.

SLEEP DEPRIVATION

You've probably heard it before—"Get your eight hours of sleep," they say. But how many of us actually do? The truth is, in our fast-paced, always-on world, sleep has become one of the first things we sacrifice. We push ourselves to stay up later, wake up earlier, and somehow, we think we can get away with it. But the reality is catching up with us, and it's not pretty.

According to the National Sleep Foundation, most adults need a solid seven to eight hours of sleep each night to feel truly alert and refreshed. Sure, there are a few rare individuals who can thrive on less, but for the vast majority of us, cutting corners on sleep is a recipe for disaster. And the numbers don't lie. Their latest report on America's sleep habits paints a troubling picture: about 40% of Americans unintentionally fall asleep during the day at least once a month. Even more alarming, 5% admit to nodding off while driving. Just think about that—a significant portion of the population is so sleep-deprived that they're dozing off behind the wheel.

But the consequences of not getting enough sleep go far beyond just feeling tired. Chronic sleep deprivation has been linked to a slew of serious health problems, including diabetes, cardiovascular disease, obesity, and depression. Over the years, as more and more adults report getting less than the recommended seven hours of sleep, we've seen a corresponding rise in these conditions. It's not just a coincidence—there's a strong connection between poor sleep and declining health.

What's more, the impact of insufficient sleep isn't just limited to the individual. When we don't get enough rest, it affects our ability to function at work, our relationships with others, and our overall quality of life. The ripple effects spread through society, impacting productivity, healthcare costs, and even public safety. It's clear that this isn't just a personal issue—it's a public health crisis.

Now, you might be thinking, "I'll catch up on sleep when I'm older." But here's the kicker—our need for sleep actually increases as we age. Research shows that the aging process brings about changes in our sleep patterns, making it harder to achieve deep, restorative sleep. Older adults often experience more wakefulness during the night, and while these changes are normal, they don't make sleep any less important. In fact, it's just the opposite.

As we age, sleep becomes even more critical to our overall health and well-being. It's during sleep that our bodies undergo essential processes of healing and rejuvenation. Quality sleep supports cognitive function, memory consolidation, and emotional stability. It helps strengthen our immune system, making us more resilient to infections and diseases. And it's not just about avoiding chronic conditions like heart disease or diabetes—adequate sleep also plays a crucial role in maintaining mental health, reducing the risk of depression, and enhancing our quality of life.

So, what can we do about it? First and foremost, we need to start taking sleep seriously. This means establishing a regular sleep routine, creating a comfortable and peaceful sleep environment, and practicing good sleep hygiene. Avoid stimulating activities before bedtime—ditch the late-night screen time, manage your stress, and be mindful of what you eat and drink in the hours leading up to sleep.

For older adults, these practices are especially important. The body's natural changes in sleep patterns can make it harder to get the rest you need, but by prioritizing sleep, you can improve your health and vitality well into your later years. Remember, it's not just about the number of hours you spend in bed—it's about the quality of that sleep.

We often underestimate the power of a good night's sleep, but it's one of the most important things we can do for our health. Whether you're young or old, making sleep a priority is key to living a vibrant, fulfilling life. So tonight, turn off the TV, put your phone on silent, and give yourself the gift of rest. Your body and mind will thank you.

ATTENTION FRAGMENTATION

We live in an era where sitting quietly with our imperfections is almost unheard of. Alain de Botton, in his thought-provoking book *The Art of Travel*, suggests that accepting our flaws might lead us to a more authentic way of being. Yet, our society idolizes perfection and views flaws as weaknesses, creating a paradox where striving for constant perfection leads to a fragmented attention span and processing anxiety. This issue, termed "attention fragmentation" by Palmer, is often the elephant in the room—the root cause of our inability to focus.

In today's world, the relentless demands on our attention come from all directions. Our phones buzz with notifications, our to-do lists grow longer, and our minds are constantly pulled in multiple directions. This leaves us feeling overwhelmed and unable to fully engage with any one task. Concentration is a limited resource, and our selective attention is constantly under siege. Each new task or distraction swamps our ability to center ourselves, robbing us of the opportunity to experience true, undivided attention. This fragmented state of mind not only hampers our productivity but also erodes our sense of self, often leading to feelings of inadequacy and self-disgust.

Let's take a moment to consider Percy's viewpoint. While there's some merit to the argument that attention fragmentation is a byproduct of modern society's relentless pace, it's also essential to recognize how this phenomenon affects our daily lives and overall well-being. We can all relate to the experience of trying to juggle multiple tasks at once, only to end up feeling scattered and unfulfilled. The pervasive influence of technology and the constant stream of information contribute significantly to this state of distraction.

Think about a typical day: You're working on an important project when your phone buzzes with a notification. You check it, then another, and before you know it, you've spent 20 minutes scrolling through social media. When you finally return to your work, you've lost your flow, and it takes time to regain your focus. This cycle repeats itself throughout the day, leaving you feeling exhausted and frustrated by the end.

Throughout history, societies have always had to balance work and leisure. The expectation of how we should spend our time has been closely linked to economic production. In the past, leisure time was often a clear and distinct part of life, separate from work. However, the lines between production, freedom, and leisure have become increasingly blurred, especially for the so-called "anxious generation." This blurring is both a cause and a consequence of the pervasive attention fragmentation we experience today.

The anxious generation, constantly seeking to escape this overwhelming fragmentation, often turns to the classics of adventure travel. These stories offer a refuge, a way to reclaim a sense of purpose and fulfillment. By immersing themselves in tales of exploration and discovery, individuals attempt to regain their focus and attention. Take, for example, the resurgence in popularity of books like Jack Kerouac's *On the Road*. This classic, with its themes of adventure and self-discovery, resonates with those looking to break free from the relentless demands of modern life.

However, finding solace in adventure stories isn't enough to address the root of attention fragmentation. We need to create spaces in our lives for genuine connection and undistracted focus. This might mean setting boundaries with technology, carving out time for activities that require sustained attention, and practicing mindfulness to ground ourselves in the present moment.

Consider incorporating habits that promote deeper engagement and reduce distraction. Start by designating specific times for checking emails and social media, rather than allowing them to interrupt your day constantly. Create a work environment that minimizes distractions, perhaps by using noise-canceling headphones or working in a quiet space. Engage in activities that naturally demand your full attention, such as reading a book, playing a musical instrument, or engaging in a meaningful conversation with a friend.

By challenging the fragmented state of attention and embracing our imperfections, we can find a deeper connection with ourselves and the world around us. It's about reclaiming our ability to focus, to give our full attention to the moment, and to appreciate the beauty in our imperfections. In doing so, we not only improve our productivity and well-being but also enhance our capacity for genuine human connection.

In conclusion, attention fragmentation is a significant challenge of our time, exacerbated by the relentless pace of modern life and the constant presence of digital distractions. By acknowledging this issue and taking proactive steps to manage our attention, we can break free from the cycle of distraction and rediscover a sense of fulfillment and purpose. Embracing the wisdom found in classic adventure tales and implementing mindful practices can help us navigate this fragmented world with greater clarity and intention.

SOCIAL MEDIA ADDICTION

In today's world, the fear of missing out (FOMO) and the pressure to stay constantly engaged with social media have made it increasingly difficult to maintain a healthy balance. We're bombarded with notifications, requests, and updates, pulling us into an endless cycle of digital interaction. This constant influx of information compels us to chase experiences that bring immediate gratification, often at the cost of our mental well-being. It's crucial to understand that these platforms are not neutral—they are meticulously designed to hook us, keeping us engaged with the bare minimum effort to mitigate their harmful effects, such as misinformation and manipulation.

The business model behind social media thrives on our need for social validation. As we scroll, like, and share, we feed a profit-driven machine exploiting our psychological vulnerabilities. This system is built to keep us coming back, often leading us to sacrifice our autonomy. We become unwitting contributors, spending our time and energy maintaining these platforms, much like workers who feel trapped in a job they cannot escape. This leads to a kind of decision fatigue that leaves us mentally exhausted.

Social media addiction is more than just a personal struggle; it's a societal issue with far-reaching consequences. It is pervasive and insidious, and its impact on society cannot be underestimated. What began as a simple way to connect with friends and share life's moments has evolved into a complex web of expectations, social norms, and constant engagement. Every notification tugs at our attention, draining our limited resources of time and energy and often leaving us feeling more disconnected than connected.

Let's consider Madison, a 28-year-old marketing professional. Her day starts with a quick check of Instagram, but that quick check often turns into an hour-long scroll through photos, videos, and updates from friends and influencers. She reaches for her phone whenever she has a spare moment—while waiting for her coffee, during a lull at work, or even in the bathroom. By the end of the day, she's exhausted from her job and constant engagement with social media. She feels drained, yet she can't stop herself from checking her phone just once more before bed. Madison's experience is far from unique. It reflects the reality of millions of people who find themselves trapped in a cycle of social media addiction.

Or take the example of Tom, a college student who relies heavily on social media to stay connected with his peers. Tom spends hours daily on platforms like Twitter and TikTok for entertainment and to stay informed about what's happening worldwide. However, this constant connection comes at a cost. Tom often feels overwhelmed by the sheer volume of information and opinions he encounters online. He struggles with anxiety, feeling like he's constantly behind or missing out on important events. Despite recognizing the negative impact on his mental health, Tom finds it difficult to cut back on his social media use because he fears being left out or uninformed.

These examples illustrate how social media addiction can infiltrate our daily lives, affecting not only our productivity and mental health but also our overall quality of life. The endless scroll and constant connection may give us the illusion of control, but we're often at the mercy of these platforms, designed to keep us hooked.

In an age of information overload, we're faced with an overwhelming number of choices, each demanding our attention. The endless stream of content assaults our senses, tearing us between the desire to stay informed and the need to protect our mental health. The temptation to lose ourselves in mindless scrolling and virtual validation strengthens as we seek belonging and connection in a world that often feels increasingly fragmented.

Social media platforms are engineered to exploit our psychological vulnerabilities. They tap into our deep-seated need for social approval and connection, using sophisticated algorithms to keep us engaged. These platforms are designed to deliver intermittent rewards, much like a slot machine, making it difficult to predict when we'll receive the next "hit" of validation in the form of likes, comments, or shares. This unpredictability keeps us returning for more, even when we know that the experience often leaves us feeling empty or anxious.

The constant comparison that social media fosters also takes a toll on our mental health. Scrolling through carefully curated images and highlighting reels of other people's lives makes it easy to feel inadequate or unfulfilled. This comparison trap can lead to feelings of jealousy, low self-esteem, and even depression. In extreme cases, it can contribute to the development of body image issues, particularly among young people who are still developing their sense of self.

Overcoming social media addiction is not easy, particularly in a world where these platforms are so deeply integrated into our daily lives. One of the biggest challenges is that social media has become many people's primary means of communication. It's how we stay in touch with friends and family, network professionally, and remain informed about the world. The fear of missing out on important connections or information can make stepping away from social media difficult, even when we know it's hurting our lives.

Another challenge is the social pressure to stay connected. For many people, social media is not just a tool for communication—it's a social obligation. There's an expectation that we'll be constantly available, that we'll respond quickly to messages, and that we'll keep our profiles updated with the latest photos and posts. This pressure to perform and conform can make setting boundaries or taking a break from social media difficult.

The design of social media platforms themselves also presents a significant challenge. These platforms are intentionally designed to be addictive, using features like infinite scroll, autoplay videos, and notifications to keep us engaged. Even when we're aware of these manipulative tactics, it can be difficult to resist the pull of social media, particularly when we're bored, lonely, or seeking distraction.

Despite the challenges, it is possible to regain control over social media use and develop a healthier relationship with these platforms. The first step is to cultivate awareness about social media's impact on our lives. This involves paying attention to how we feel before, during, and after using social media. Are we using it to connect with others meaningfully, or are we using it to fill a void or distract ourselves from other problems? By reflecting on our motivations and the effects of our social media use, we can begin to make more intentional choices about how and when we engage with these platforms.

Setting boundaries is another crucial step. This might involve setting specific times of day when you check social media, limiting your time on these platforms, or turning off notifications so that you're not constantly interrupted. It might be helpful for some people to take regular breaks from social media, such as a "digital detox," where you step away from all online platforms for a set period. These breaks can help to reset your relationship with social media and give you the space to focus on other areas of your life.

It's also important to curate your social media experience to support your well-being. This might involve unfollowing accounts that make you feel anxious or inadequate, following accounts that inspire and uplift you, or setting up filters to limit the amount of negative content you're exposed to. Taking control of what you see on social media can create a more positive and empowering experience.

Another effective strategy is to replace social media with other activities that fulfill your needs for connection and entertainment. This might involve hobbies, connecting with friends and family, or participating in offline communities. Finding alternative sources of fulfillment can reduce your reliance on social media and create a more balanced life.

Finally, it's important to advocate for change at a broader level. This involves holding social media companies accountable for their platforms' impact on users. We can push for greater transparency in how these platforms operate, demand stronger regulations to protect user privacy and mental health, and support initiatives that promote digital literacy and healthy online behavior.

As we work to overcome social media addiction, we must remember the value of authentic, face-to-face connection; in a world that often prioritizes online interaction, making an effort to connect with others in person can be a powerful antidote to the isolation and anxiety social media can foster. Whether spending time with loved ones, participating in community events, or conversing with friends, these real-world connections can help ground us and remind us of what truly matters.

Reclaiming our attention and energy from social media is not just about reducing our screen time—it's about rethinking how we engage with the digital world. It's about recognizing how these platforms shape our thoughts, feelings, and behaviors and consciously deciding to take back control. By cultivating awareness, setting boundaries, and seeking meaningful connections, we can create a healthier and more balanced relationship with social media that enhances our lives rather than detracts from them.

Social media addiction is a complex and pervasive issue that affects millions of people worldwide. While these platforms offer valuable opportunities for connection and communication, they also pose significant risks to our mental health and well-being. By understanding the psychological mechanisms behind social media addiction and taking proactive steps to manage our digital lives, we can break free from the cycle of excessive engagement and create a more fulfilling and balanced existence.

Ultimately, the key to overcoming social media addiction lies in reclaiming our autonomy and agency. It's about recognizing that we can choose how we engage with the digital world and make decisions that align with our values and well-being. Through awareness, intentionality, and a commitment to authentic connection, we can navigate the complexities of social media.

LONELINESS AND SOCIAL CONTAGION

We've all felt that quiet, creeping sense of loneliness that seems to hang over our generation like a shadow. For millennials, born between the early 1980s and the mid-1990s, loneliness isn't just a passing mood; it's a defining feature of our experience. Sociologists and economists have pointed to us as the generation most afflicted by loneliness, and there's a mountain of research to back that up. It's ironic. We're the most connected generation in history, yet we often feel more disconnected than ever before.

It's hard to pinpoint exactly when it happened, but somewhere along the way, social media became more than just a tool for staying in touch—it became a way of life. We poured our time and energy into creating and curating our identities online, building profiles that we hoped would reflect our true selves. But in doing so, we inadvertently sacrificed something far more important: our real-world connections.

The natural, unfiltered exchanges essential to feeling truly seen, heard, and understood became increasingly rare. Instead of face-to-face conversations, we communicated through screens, our words filtered through text, our emotions conveyed by emojis. What was once a genuine connection became a transaction—likes for likes, follows for follows. The more time we spend online, the less we engage in the physical world. We became more connected to our devices and less connected to each other.

This shift affected our personal lives and seeped into our professional lives as well. Remote work, once a novelty, became the norm. Once a social interaction hub, Zoom calls and Slack messages replaced the office. The spontaneous conversations that sparked creativity and camaraderie were replaced by carefully scheduled meetings, leaving little room for the organic connection that builds strong relationships.

Despite the undeniable convenience of these technological advancements, the unintended consequence was an epidemic of loneliness. We turned to social media for validation, for a sense of belonging, but what we found instead was a hollow imitation of connection. Sure, we could interact with hundreds, even thousands of people at once, but those interactions often needed to be deeper, leaving us feeling more isolated than ever.

It's a bizarre twist of fate: the platforms that promised to bring us closer together drove us apart. In our quest for online validation, we lost sight of the importance of real, in-person relationships. We became so focused on maintaining our digital personas that we neglected the connections that truly matter.

But we're starting to wake up to this reality. There's a growing awareness among millennials that something has gone wrong. We're beginning to see the cracks in the facade, the emptiness behind the endless scrolling and liking. We're realizing that no amount of virtual interaction can replace the warmth of a face-to-face conversation, the comfort of a hug, or the joy of shared laughter.

In response, there's been a push to reconnect with the fundamental essence of human connection. We're stepping away from our screens and seeking real-world interactions. We're attending more in-person events, reconnecting with old friends, and trying to be present. We're trying to reclaim the sense of togetherness we lost in the digital age.

But it's not easy. Social media's pull is strong, and the habits we've developed are hard to break. Finding the balance between digital engagement and authentic face-to-face interaction is a constant struggle. We're navigating a complex landscape of social dynamics, technological advancements, and personal fulfillment, all while trying to maintain our sanity in an increasingly chaotic world.

One of the biggest challenges we face is the fear of missing out. We've been conditioned to believe that we must be constantly connected, updated, and in the know. This fear is deeply ingrained in our generation, fueled by the endless content that floods our social media feeds. But the truth is, the more we try to stay connected online, the more disconnected we become in real life.

Another challenge is the pressure to maintain our online identities. We've spent years building our profiles, curating our images, and crafting our narratives. It's hard to let go of that, even when we know it's unhealthy. We fear that stepping away from social media will mean losing our place in the digital world, losing our connection to others, and ultimately, losing ourselves.

But despite these challenges, there's a growing movement among millennials to reclaim our time, attention, and relationships. We're seeing the value in unplugging, removing social media noise, and reconnecting with the people and experiences that truly matter.

We're also beginning to recognize the importance of setting boundaries. We're learning to say no to our devices' endless demands, carve out time for ourselves, and prioritize our mental health. We realize missing the latest trend, meme, or news is okay. What matters more is the quality of our relationships, the depth of our connections, and the richness of our lives.

As we navigate this journey, we're also becoming more aware of social media's role in perpetuating loneliness. We're starting to see how these platforms, designed to keep us hooked, can make us feel more isolated. The constant comparison, the pressure to perform, and the endless pursuit of validation can take a toll on our mental health, leading to feelings of inadequacy, anxiety, and depression.

But we're not giving up. We're fighting back against the forces that seek to divide us, and we're finding new ways to connect online and offline. We're using social media more intentionally, seeking content that inspires, uplifts us, and brings us closer to our true selves. We're also creating spaces for real, meaningful interaction where we can share our stories, struggles, and successes without fearing judgment.

In the process, we're redefining what it means to be connected in the digital age. We're learning that true connection isn't about our number of followers, likes, or views. It's about the quality of our relationships, the authenticity of our interactions, and the depth of our connections.

We're also realizing that loneliness isn't just a personal problem; it's a societal issue that needs to be addressed. We're advocating for changes in how we use technology, design our workspaces, and build our communities. We're pushing for more opportunities for face-to-face interaction, more support for mental health, and more recognition of the importance of human connection.

Millennials are reclaiming their place in a rapidly evolving society through introspection, resilience, and a profound understanding of the importance of human bonds. We're on a mission to redefine social interaction, ensuring that the digital realm complements, rather than replaces, the invaluable richness of real-world connections. As we continue to navigate this ever-changing landscape, we're sparking a paradigm shift that has the power to redefine what it means to be truly connected in the modern world.

Ultimately, we're beginning to understand that the solution to loneliness isn't found in the digital world but in the real world. It's found in the people we love, the communities we build, and the connections we cultivate. It's found in the moments of vulnerability, the shared experiences, and the deep, meaningful conversations that remind us that we're not alone.

As we move forward, we must continue to challenge the status quo, push back against the forces that seek to divide us and build a future where technology serves us rather than controls us. We must strive to create a world where loneliness is the exception, not the norm, and every individual feels seen, heard, and truly connected.

SOCIAL COMPARISON AND PERFECTIONISM

In a society driven by the need for social connections and the unending quest for acceptance and validation, it's easy to fall into a vicious cycle of self-doubt and self-criticism. As a teenager, navigating the choppy waters of societal expectations can feel overwhelming. We often find ourselves seeking solace and guidance in the fleeting world of social media, where every post and every like seems to dictate our worth. From comparing our grades on tough exams to obsessing over social status, we unknowingly sacrifice our intrinsic value on the altar of external validation.

Day after day, my thoughts become fixated on the surface-level aspects of life. I worry endlessly about my appearance, especially during adolescence when physical looks carry so much weight. It's a time when every imperfection feels like a glaring flaw. The societal beauty standards we're bombarded with make us believe that if we can conform, we'll somehow win this relentless battle against ourselves.

In this age of constant connectivity, with information at our fingertips, the pressure only grows. The rise of the internet and the ever-present influence of our peers and educators amplify our insecurities. Instead of listening to voices of reason and compassion, I find myself drawn to those that fuel my self-doubt. These voices, like sirens, lure me deeper into the abyss of comparison, making it harder to remember who I truly am.

Even the smallest events can significantly impact our fragile sense of self. I remember meticulously planning my outfit for a party, only to arrive and see someone else wearing the same thing. It might seem trivial, but it stung. Initially, I tried to brush it off, but the silent regret settled in over time, chipping away at my perception of my uniqueness and elegance. It left me feeling undeserving and diminished.

We're trapped in an endless cycle of comparison and self-inflicted suffering. Our worth becomes inextricably tied to the opinions of others, and we lose sight of our unique value. But if we step back and embrace our individuality, we can break free from this destructive pattern. It's crucial to celebrate our journey rather than measure it against the distorted yardstick of societal expectations. Only then can we truly become the awe-inspiring individuals we were meant to be?

As we long to fit in and be accepted by our peers, it's easy to fall into despair and hopelessness. This despair stems from the fear that no one else shares our struggles, which profoundly impacts our self-worth, especially during adolescence. Unfortunately, this vulnerability to depression becomes even more pronounced as we try to navigate these social pressures.

The social structure we live in perpetuates this cycle of insecurity and anxiety. As the importance of our connections and associations grows in Western societies, so does our level of anxiety. Research has shown that our perceived social standing can directly impact our mental health. For example, studies among Canadian college students revealed that those who felt better about their social standing were more likely to be enrolled in college.

However, within the confines of university life, a different picture emerges. Among undergraduates in the psychology department, students from privileged economic backgrounds often face immense pressure to succeed compared to their peers. This pressure stems from various factors that create a challenging and demanding academic environment. Interestingly, despite these pressures, the influence of social associations on the manifestation of depression or anxiety symptoms wasn't as pronounced.

Further studies, like *The Year of Distress* and various college surveys, highlight the close relationship between anxiety and the pressures within the university setting. These findings prompt us to question whether these results reflect the universities' inability to support students' mental well-being adequately or if students naturally inclined to seek understanding are more likely to participate in such studies.

As we grapple with these pressures, we must recognize that our struggles with social comparison and perfectionism are part of a broader societal issue. The constant bombardment of idealized images and success stories on social media can create a distorted view of reality. We see only the highlights of others' lives, not the struggles and failures that everyone experiences. This skewed perspective can make us feel inadequate and drive us to strive for an unattainable level of perfection.

But it's important to remember that perfection is an illusion. Everyone has their unique journey, complete with ups and downs. Embracing our imperfections and learning to value our intrinsic worth can help us break free from the comparison cycle. It's about finding balance and recognizing that our worth isn't determined by how we measure up to others but by our actions, values, and personal growth.

To navigate this journey, we need to build a strong support system. Surrounding ourselves with friends and family who uplift and encourage us can make a significant difference. It's also crucial to practice self-compassion and mindfulness. Reflecting on our thoughts and feelings without judgment can help us understand our triggers and develop healthier coping mechanisms.

Educational institutions also have a role to play. They can help students manage stress and anxiety by fostering a supportive and inclusive environment. Offering mental health resources, promoting open discussions about student pressures, and creating opportunities for real, meaningful connections can all contribute to better mental health outcomes.

Ultimately, overcoming the challenges of social comparison and perfectionism requires a collective effort. It's about changing the narrative from relentless competition and external validation to self-acceptance and personal growth. By focusing on our journey and valuing our unique contributions, we can find a fulfillment and purpose that transcends societal expectations.

Digital Detox Strategy:

Create Your Own Space Rule:

✓ Designate specific times or areas where digital devices are not allowed in your daily routine. This could be during meals, bedtime, or personal relaxation time.

No Phones Before Bed Rule:

✓ Avoid screen time at least 30 minutes before bedtime to promote relaxation and prepare your mind for sleep.

Start with Small Periods:

✓ Begin your digital detox journey by gradually reducing screen time. Start with short breaks throughout the day and gradually increase the duration.

Keep Your Digital Detox Power Dry (Phase 1 Mode):

✓ During this phase, focus on reducing unnecessary digital interactions. Limit social media browsing and prioritize face-to-face interactions whenever possible.

Complete a Digital Detox Makeover (Phase 2 Mode):

✓ Take a more comprehensive approach by evaluating all digital interactions. Consider decluttering digital spaces, unfollowing accounts that don't add value, and setting stricter time limits for app usage.

Digital Detox Recovery Phase (Phase 3 Mode):

✓ Reflect on your digital detox journey and identify areas for continued improvement. Set long-term goals for maintaining a healthy balance between digital engagement and real-life interactions.

Sleep Hygiene Plan:
Conditions that Encourage and Lead to Sleep:

Identify factors contributing to a restful sleep environment, such as maintaining a consistent sleep schedule, creating a calming bedtime routine, and optimizing your sleep environment (e.g., comfortable bedding, dark and quiet room).

_____

_____

_____

_____

_____

Conditions that Provide Rest or Relaxation:

List activities or practices that help you unwind and relax before bedtime, such as reading a book, practicing relaxation techniques like deep breathing, or taking a warm bath. How do these activities contribute to improving the quality of your sleep and overall mental health?"

_____

_____

_____

_____

_____

_____

_____

Conditions that Typically Prevent or Inhibit Sleep:

Recognize habits or behaviors that disrupt your sleep, such as excessive screen time before bed, consuming caffeine late in the day, or irregular sleep patterns. How do these habits impact your overall mental health and well-being?"

_____

_____

_____

_____

_____

Sleep Schedule:

"Do you maintain a consistent sleep schedule, going to bed and waking up at the same time every day, even on weekends? Reflect on how this consistency, or lack thereof, affects your sleep quality and overall well-being."

_____

_____

_____

_____

_____

_____

"How do irregular sleep patterns or late-night activities affect your ability to fall asleep and wake up feeling rested? Reflect on how these patterns impact your overall energy levels, mood, and mental health throughout the day."

_____

_____

_____

_____

_____

Bedtime Routine:

What activities do you typically engage in before bedtime? Are they calming and conducive to sleep or stimulate your mind?

_____

_____

_____

_____

How can you improve your bedtime routine to promote relaxation and signal your body that it's time to wind down?

_____

_____

_____

_____

Sleep Environment:

Is your bedroom conducive to sleep? Consider factors like temperature, lighting, noise levels, and comfort of your mattress and bedding.

_____

_____

_____

_____

_____

Are there adjustments you can make to create a more sleep-friendly environment?

_____

_____

_____

_____

_____

Tips for Creating Your Plans:

Personalization: Tailor your sleep hygiene and digital detox plans to fit your needs and preferences. Consider the most essential components and how to implement them effectively.

Reflection: Reflect on how your current habits impact your sleep and wellbeing. Identify areas where you can make small changes for improvement.

CHAPTER FOUR
GENDER DIFFERENCES IN MENTAL HEALTH IMPACT

"Understanding gender differences in mental health is key to developing tailored interventions that can more effectively support each individual's unique needs." - Susan Nolen-Hoeksema

Growing up in today's world can feel like being caught in a whirlwind of emotions and expectations, especially when it comes to how we deal with mental health. As teenagers, we're often told that boys and girls are just different—they think differently, feel differently, and even suffer differently. But what does that mean for us, the so-called "anxious generation"? How do these differences shape the way we experience things like anxiety, depression, and stress? And more importantly, how can we learn to cope in a world that sometimes feels like it's trying to pull us apart?

It's no secret that girls and boys often handle things differently. Ever since people started paying attention to mental health, there's been a lot of talk about whether there's a "feminine" and a "masculine" way of dealing with problems. Terms like "penis envy," "maternal instinct," and "castration complex" might sound outdated or even silly, but they were once used to try and explain why men and women think and act the way they do. Freud and other early psychologists were obsessed with these ideas, trying to map out a "psychic anatomy" that could explain our inner worlds.

But here's the thing: while it's true that boys and girls might face different pressures, we're all navigating the same chaotic, digital world. And in this world, social media, peer pressure, and academic stress don't discriminate—they hit us all hard in different ways.

Take, for instance, the way girls and boys handle stress. Girls are often more likely to talk about their feelings. Maybe it's because we're encouraged to be open and expressive, or perhaps it's just because we feel the pressure to be perfect, always to have it all together. On social media, it can feel like everyone else is managing just fine while we're the only ones struggling. This can make us feel even more isolated, even though friends and followers surround us.

Conversely, boys might not talk about their feelings as much, but that doesn't mean they're not struggling. They might channel their stress into activities—playing sports, working out, or even diving into video games to escape. The problem is that these coping mechanisms can sometimes mask deeper issues. When society expects boys to be strong and stoic, they might feel like they can't show vulnerability, even when they're hurting inside.

Let's consider an example that many of us can relate to. Imagine you're at school, and everyone's talking about their grades after a big test. For some of us, hearing about other people's successes can feel like a punch to the gut, especially if we didn't do as well. It's easy to fall into the trap of comparing ourselves to others, thinking that we're not good enough I'll never measure up. This kind of comparison can be brutal, and it's something that affects both girls and boys, just in different ways.

For girls, this might translate into anxiety and perfectionism. We might start to feel like we have to be perfect in everything we do— our grades, appearance, and social lives. And when we inevitably fall short, it can feel like the world is crashing down around us. This pressure to be perfect is something that's deeply ingrained in our culture, and it can take a serious toll on our mental health.

For boys, the pressure might manifest differently. Instead of striving for perfection, they might need to prove themselves in other ways—through sports, social dominance, or by suppressing their emotions. This can lead to a whole different set of problems, like anger issues, substance abuse, or even depression. But because boys are often taught to "man up" and keep their emotions in check, they might not even realize they're struggling until it's too late.

The digital world we live in only makes these pressures worse. Social media creates an endless cycle of comparison, where we're constantly bombarded with images of other people's seemingly perfect lives. It's easy to forget that these images are often carefully curated, showing only the best moments and leaving out the struggles. But when scrolling through our feeds, it's hard not to feel like we're the only ones who don't have it all together.

As part of the "anxious generation," we're facing challenges our parents and grandparents never had to deal with. The rise of social media has created a whole new landscape for mental health, one where anxiety, depression, and stress are almost expected. But that doesn't mean we're doomed to suffer. By understanding the ways that gender impacts our mental health, we can start to develop better-coping strategies and support each other in more meaningful ways.

For instance, if you're a girl who struggles with anxiety or perfectionism, it might help to remember that you don't have to be perfect. It's okay to have flaws, make mistakes, and ask for help when needed. Surround yourself with people who lift you and remind you of your worth, not just those who add to the pressure.

If you're a boy who feels like you can't show your emotions, know it's okay to be vulnerable. You don't have to carry the world's weight on your shoulders. Talk to someone you trust—a friend, a parent, or a therapist—about what you're going through. It's not a sign of weakness; it's a sign of strength.

As teenagers, we're all trying to figure out who we are and where we fit. It's a tough journey, made even tougher by the pressures we face from every direction. However, by understanding the unique challenges of being a part of the "anxious generation," we can start building a community that supports each other, regardless of gender.

This means breaking down the stereotypes that tell us how we're supposed to act and feel. It means recognizing that mental health is a complex issue that affects everyone differently and that there's no one-size-fits-all solution. Most importantly, it means being there for each other—whether by lending an ear, offering a kind word, or simply being present when someone needs you.

In a world that often feels like it's moving too fast, it's easy to get caught up in the noise. But if we take a step back and focus on what matters—our connections with each other, our mental health, and our personal growth—we can start to navigate these challenges with more confidence and resilience.

The gender differences in mental health are real, but they don't have to define us. By understanding these differences and working together to support each other, we can break free from the expectations that hold us back and create a brighter, healthier future for ourselves and the generations to come.

Ultimately, it's about finding balance—between who we are and who we're expected to be, between our online lives and real lives, and between the pressures we face and the support we give each other.

WHY SOCIAL MEDIA DAMAGES GIRLS MORE

When you sit down with a group of teenage girls and ask about their experiences with Instagram, you'll likely get a range of reactions—some good, some bad. Most will admit that while Instagram has its perks, it also stirs up a lot of anxiety and worry. They talk about the constant pressure to stay in the loop, the fear of missing out (FOMO), and the stress of always putting their best foot forward. It's not just a casual concern; the stakes feel incredibly high for many girls. They're worried about what others are doing, who they hang out with, and how they are perceived. This constant comparison and the need to present a flawless image can be exhausting and damaging, especially for young girls still figuring out who they are.

Why Social Media Hurts Girls More

The impact of social media on teenage girls is profound, and it's rooted in a few key reasons:

❖ **Pressure to Conform to Unrealistic Standards**: Social media platforms like Instagram are filled with images of perfection. The pressure to conform to these unrealistic standards is intense, whether it's beauty, body image, or lifestyle. Teenage girls at a critical stage of developing their self-identity are particularly vulnerable to these pressures. They often see the edited, filtered, and curated versions of others' lives and feel they must measure up without realizing that what they see isn't real life.

❖ **Comparison Culture**: Social media encourages constant comparison. For teenage girls, this can lead to feelings of inadequacy and low self-esteem. They're comparing their behind-the-scenes with everyone else's highlight reel, and it's a battle they're destined to lose. The number of likes, followers, and comments becomes a measure of self-worth, leading to anxiety and a relentless need for validation.

❖ **Cyberbullying and Online Harassment**: Unfortunately, social media platforms can also be breeding grounds for bullying and harassment. Teenage girls are often targets of cruel comments, body shaming, and even more severe forms of online abuse. The anonymity and reach of social media make it easier for bullies to attack without facing immediate consequences, leaving the victims feeling powerless and isolated.

❖ **Fear of Missing Out (FOMO)**: Another significant factor is the fear of missing out. Girls may think that if they're not constantly online, they'll miss something important or be left out of social circles. This leads to a compulsive need to check their feeds, stay updated on every post, and ensure they're not missing out on what's happening in their friends' lives.

Challenges and Struggles

The challenges that teenage girls face on social media are complex and multifaceted:

❖ **Mental Health Impact**: The pressure to maintain a perfect online image can lead to anxiety, depression, and other mental health issues. Girls may become obsessed with their appearance, popularity, and the feedback they receive on their posts, which can be emotionally draining.

❖ **Distorted Self-Image**: Constant exposure to edited and filtered images can distort girls' perceptions of their bodies. They might start to believe that they're not good enough or that they need to change how they look to fit in, leading to body dissatisfaction and, in some cases, eating disorders.

❖ **Isolation and Loneliness**: Social media is supposed to connect people, but it can often have the opposite effect. Girls might feel isolated if they don't receive the same attention as their peers or perceive that their lives aren't as exciting or glamorous. This can lead to feelings of loneliness and social disconnection.

❖ **Addiction and Overuse**: Social media platforms are designed to be addictive. The constant notifications, the endless scroll, and the instant gratification of likes and comments can make it hard for girls to disconnect. This can lead to overuse, which in turn exacerbates the negative mental health effects.

Examples

Consider a 14-year-old girl named Lily. Every morning, the first thing Lily does is check Instagram. She's not just catching up on what she missed overnight—she's also checking to see how many likes her latest post received, comparing herself to the influencers she follows, and worrying about why her friend didn't comment on her picture. Throughout the day, Lily feels a constant pressure to look perfect, to post something that will get attention, and to stay relevant in her social circles. By the time she goes to bed, she's emotionally exhausted, but she still finds herself scrolling through her feed, unable to disconnect.

Then there's Emma, a 16-year-old who has always been confident and outgoing. But after a few mean comments on her photos, she doubts herself. She begins to withdraw, editing her pictures more and more before posting them and spending hours trying to craft the perfect caption. The negative feedback she receives online begins to affect her self-esteem, and she starts to feel like she can't live up to the expectations set by her peers. Emma's once bright personality dims as she becomes more concerned with fitting in and less sure of who she is.

Solutions

While the challenges are significant, some steps can be taken to help teenage girls navigate the digital landscape more safely and healthily:

❖ **Education and Awareness**: One of the most important steps is educating girls about the realities of social media. This includes teaching them that what they see online isn't always real and that taking breaks from social media is okay. Parents, educators, and mental health professionals can play a key role in helping girls understand the impact of social media on their mental health and self-esteem.

❖ **Encouraging Offline Activities**: Encouraging girls to engage in activities outside of social media can help them develop a more balanced lifestyle. This could include sports, hobbies, or spending time with friends and family in person. These activities can help girls build self-esteem, reduce stress, and form meaningful connections.

❖ **Promoting Positive Role Models**: Instead of following influencers who promote unrealistic beauty standards or materialism, girls should be encouraged to follow positive role models who promote self-acceptance, kindness, and healthy living. These role models can provide a counterbalance to the negative messages that are often prevalent on social media.

❖ **Setting Boundaries**: Girls need to set boundaries around their social media use. This could mean limiting their time on these platforms, turning off notifications, or deciding not to engage in certain types of online behavior. Setting these boundaries can help girls take control of their social media experience rather than letting it control them.

❖ **Parental Guidance and Support**: Parents play a crucial role in helping their children navigate social media. This includes having open conversations about the pressures of social media, monitoring their children's online activity, and being a source of support if their child is struggling. Parents should also model healthy social media habits themselves.

❖ **Mental Health Resources**: Providing access to mental health resources is vital. This could include school counselors, support groups, or therapy. If a girl is struggling with the pressures of social media, having someone to talk to can make a significant difference.

Social media is a powerful tool, but it needs to be used with care—especially for teenage girls. While platforms like Instagram offer opportunities for connection and self-expression, they also bring challenges that can be damaging if not managed properly. By understanding these challenges, providing education and support, and promoting healthier ways to engage with social media, we can help girls navigate this complex digital landscape with confidence and resilience.

The goal is to shift the relationship with social media from pressure and anxiety to empowerment and self-expression. Social media should be a space where girls feel free to be themselves, connect with others in meaningful ways, and find inspiration without needing to conform to unrealistic standards. By fostering a judgment-free environment that values authenticity over popularity, we can help create a digital world that truly supports the well-being of the "anxious generation."

BOYS' WITHDRAWAL INTO THE VIRTUAL WORLD

In today's fast-paced, tech-driven world, it's becoming increasingly common for boys to retreat from social interactions and immerse themselves in the virtual realm. This shift toward the digital world might seem like a harmless escape, but it's a coping mechanism that comes with significant consequences. By withdrawing into their virtual spaces, boys often find a refuge free from real-life relationships' complexities and emotional challenges. However, this escape can lead to an emotional disconnect, limited personal growth, and a fragmented understanding of the world around them.

One of the main reasons boys are drawn to the virtual world is the desire to avoid the emotional and social challenges of the real world. The digital realm offers a place where they can be in control, where interactions are more predictable, and where they can avoid the vulnerability of face-to-face communication. In this virtual space, boys can engage with technology in a compartmentalized and controlled way, offering a sense of security that is often missing in their offline lives.

This retreat is often marked by a more attenuated character structure, meaning it lacks depth and emotional range. Boys who spend excessive time in the virtual world may develop shallow interpersonal connections, as their interactions are primarily based on virtual companions rather than real-life relationships. This can lead to a limited understanding of the world, as their knowledge becomes fragmented and disconnected from the broader context of human experience.

The digital world is characterized by its obsession with speed and constant change. For many boys, this fast-paced environment is both exciting and overwhelming. The relentless pursuit of novelty can fragment their sense of self, leading to a self-centered mindset as they struggle to keep up with the ever-evolving digital landscape. This can further isolate them from meaningful relationships with family, friends, and peers as they focus more on their virtual achievements than on building real-world connections.

As boys prioritize their virtual lives, the value of authentic human connections diminishes. This shift is often driven by the demands of a depersonalized economy that values productivity and individual success over community and cooperation. In this environment, qualities such as empathy, collaboration, and self-expression are often undervalued, leading to a society that places more importance on assertiveness and high achievement.

Returning to the virtual world has profound consequences for boys, particularly how they perceive themselves and their societal place. This withdrawal can lead to a rejection of their self-image and a growing sense of alienation from their true selves. As they become more detached from their emotions and relationships with others, boys may struggle to develop the qualities essential for a fulfilling life—curiosity, devotion, openness, affection, and the ability to bring joy to others.

Interestingly, even in non-gender-specific virtual environments, such as role-playing games, implicit gender conventions persist.

These games often reinforce traditional gender roles, which can further limit boys' ability to explore different aspects of their identity. As boys transition from adolescence to adulthood, they may find themselves navigating a desolate landscape that lacks the vitality and connection they crave.

As boys spend more time in the virtual world, they may become desensitized to the emotional and social challenges of the real world. This desensitization is often accompanied by a reification of societal norms, values, and institutions, perpetuating alienation and detachment. In this context, boys learn to prioritize immediate, surface-level needs over deeper emotional and social connections. This focus on short-term gratification can gradually erode empathy and a growing sense of apathy.

The result is a numbing of the self, where boys become increasingly detached from their emotions and disconnected from the people around them. As their ability to empathize deteriorates, they may find it difficult to form meaningful relationships or to care deeply about the world around them. This emotional distance can lead to a cycle of loneliness and isolation, where boys retreat further into the virtual world to escape the pain of real-life interactions.

Examples

Consider the story of Alex, a 15-year-old boy who spends most of his free time playing online games. For Alex, the virtual world offers an escape from the pressures of school and the social dynamics that he finds overwhelming. In the game, he can be whoever he wants to be, free from the judgments of his peers. However, as Alex becomes more engrossed in his virtual life, he pulls away from his real-life friends and family. He stopped participating in activities he once enjoyed, like playing soccer or hanging out with his cousins. Over time, Alex's world becomes increasingly narrow, centered around his online persona, and disconnected from those who care about him.

Then there's Ben, a 17-year-old who has always been shy and introverted. Ben finds it difficult to express his emotions and often feels misunderstood by his parents and teachers. In the virtual world, however, Ben can communicate more freely, hiding behind the anonymity of the screen. But this anonymity comes at a cost—Ben struggles to build real-life relationships and often feels isolated and lonely. He knows virtual friends aren't the same as having someone to talk to in person, but the thought of opening up in the real world is too daunting.

Solutions

The challenges that boys face in withdrawing into the virtual world are significant. Still, steps can be taken to help them reconnect with the real world and develop healthier relationships with technology.

1. **Encouraging Balance**: It's important to encourage boys to balance their virtual and real-world lives. This means setting limits on screen time and encouraging them to engage in offline activities that promote physical, emotional, and social well-being. Sports, hobbies, and spending time with family and friends are all important ways to help boys develop a more balanced lifestyle.

2. **Promoting Emotional Intelligence**: Helping boys develop emotional intelligence is key to building stronger relationships and navigating the challenges of the real world. This includes teaching them how to recognize and express their emotions, empathize with others, and make meaningful connections. Schools and parents can play a crucial role in fostering these skills through open conversations, role-playing, and encouraging emotional expression.

3. **Building Real-World Skills**: Boys need to develop the skills that will help them succeed in the real world, such as communication, problem-solving, and teamwork. These skills are often overlooked in the virtual world, where interactions are more transactional and less collaborative. By focusing on building these skills in real-life settings, boys can learn to navigate the complexities of social interactions and develop stronger connections with others.

4. **Encouraging Mindfulness and Reflection**: Mindfulness practices can help boys become more aware of their thoughts, emotions, and behaviors, allowing them to manage their relationship with technology better. Encouraging boys to reflect on their virtual experiences and how they impact their real-world lives can help them develop a healthier perspective on technology use.

5. **Providing Support and Guidance**: Parents, teachers, and mentors play a critical role in helping boys navigate the challenges of the digital age. Providing guidance on healthy technology use, encouraging open communication, and offering support when boys struggle with social interactions can significantly affect their ability to form meaningful relationships and avoid the pitfalls of virtual withdrawal.

The retreat of boys into the virtual world is a symptom of a broader societal shift towards technology and away from face-to-face interactions. While the virtual world offers a convenient escape, it can also lead to emotional detachment, fragmented self-identity, and a diminished capacity for empathy and connection.

To address these challenges, it's essential to encourage boys to engage with the real world in meaningful ways. By fostering emotional intelligence, promoting real-world skills, and providing support and guidance, we can help boys navigate the digital landscape more effectively and build the connections essential for a fulfilling life.

SELF-REFLECTION QUESTIONS

Impact of Societal Expectations:

How have societal expectations around gender influenced your views on mental health?

_____

_____

_____

_____

Do you feel pressure to conform to specific emotional norms based on your gender?

_____

_____

_____

_____

Reflect on any experiences where you felt judged or misunderstood due to societal expectations about how your gender should express emotions or handle mental health challenges.

_____

_____

_____

_____

Family Dynamics and Expectations:

How do your family's beliefs about gender roles affect your perception of mental health?

_____

_____

_____

_____

Are specific expectations or pressures placed on you based on your gender identity?

_____

_____

_____

_____

Have you ever felt the need to hide or downplay mental health issues to avoid disappointing your family or being perceived negatively?

_____

_____

_____

_____

Personal Coping Strategies:

What strategies have you developed to cope with societal pressures related to mental health and gender norms?

_____

_____

_____

_____

Are these strategies supportive and healthy, or do they contribute to additional stress and self-doubt?

_____

_____

_____

_____

Reflect on times when you've felt conflicted between being true to yourself and conforming to societal expectations regarding mental health and gender roles.

_____

_____

_____

_____

Support Systems and Acceptance:

How do your support systems (friends, family, community) react to discussions about mental health within the context of gender norms?

_____

_____

_____

_____

Are there barriers or challenges you face in seeking support due to gender-related expectations?

_____

_____

_____

_____

Reflect on whether you feel accepted and understood when discussing mental health issues, especially those that may challenge traditional gender roles.

_____

_____

_____

_____

Exercise:

Scenario Analysis: Consider a scenario where societal gender norms clash with mental health challenges. Write a personal reflection or narrative where you explore how gender expectations influenced your perception of mental health issues and your journey toward self-acceptance and resilience.

_____

_____

_____

_____

_____

_____

_____

Role Play: Engage in a role-play exercise where you take on different gender roles in discussing mental health. Explore how each role feels pressured or supported based on societal norms and expectations.

_____

_____

_____

_____

_____

_____

_____

Media Analysis: Analyze media representations of mental health issues related to gender. How do these representations reinforce or challenge existing stereotypes? Reflect on how media portrayals impact your own beliefs about mental health and gender norms.

_____

_____

_____

_____

_____

_____

_____

Peer Discussion: Initiate a discussion with peers or support groups about their experiences with societal gender norms and mental health. Share insights and strategies for navigating these challenges while promoting understanding and acceptance.

_____

_____

_____

_____

_____

_____

_____

Chapter Note

CHAPTER FIVE
CONSEQUENCES FOR SOCIETY

"The consequences of unchecked digital dependency on society are profound, shaping how we interact, learn, and thrive in the modern age." –
Nicholas Carr

Suppose you were to sit down with a group of teenagers today and ask them about their experiences with social media, especially platforms like Instagram. In that case, you'd probably get a lot of mixed reactions. Sure, they might talk about the fun and the connection, but underneath that, there's a lot of anxiety and stress. Many of these teens, especially girls, confess that while Instagram has its perks, it also brings unease, self-doubt, and even fear. It's not just about posting pictures; it's about the pressure to constantly be on, keep up with what everyone else is doing, and present a perfect life. This isn't just a personal issue—it's affecting our entire generation in ways that reshape society.

Think about the way we use social media. For many girls, every post, every like, and every comment becomes a measure of their worth. They're constantly comparing themselves to others in terms of looks and every aspect of life. Who's hanging out with whom? Who's doing something exciting? Who's getting the most attention? This constant comparison isn't just exhausting; it's damaging. It chips away at self-esteem and creates a cycle of anxiety where the need for validation from others becomes overwhelming. And it's not just about feeling left out—it's about feeling like you're never enough, no matter how hard you try.

Even more troubling is that this kind of stress doesn't stay online. It spills over into real life, affecting how girls interact with their friends, perform in school, and even see themselves in the mirror. The pressure to maintain a flawless image, to always say the right thing, and to be liked by everyone can be crushing. It's no wonder that so many of us are feeling more anxious and depressed than ever before. The digital world that was supposed to connect us is making us feel more isolated and alone.

This problem isn't just about individual struggles; it's about how our society evolves. Mental health issues are on the rise, and they're not just affecting a few people—they're affecting a whole generation. When nearly a quarter of all health-related problems in society are linked to mental health, it's clear that something is seriously wrong. And when you consider that a lot of this stress comes from the digital world, it becomes even more concerning. We're living in a time where technology is supposed to make our lives easier, but for many of us, it's doing the opposite.

The economic impact of this mental health crisis is also huge. When people are struggling with anxiety and depression, they're less productive, they miss more school or work, and they're more likely to need healthcare. This isn't just a problem for individuals; it's a problem for the whole economy. Companies are starting to realize that they need to invest in their employees' mental health to succeed, but this recognition is still in its early stages. The systems we have in place—whether in schools, workplaces, or healthcare—aren't doing enough to support mental well-being.

The way we work and learn also contributes to this problem. In school, the pressure to perform is intense. It's not just about getting good grades; it's about getting the right grades to get into the right college, get the right job, and have the right life. And with the constant presence of social media, it feels like there's no escape from this pressure. Even when we're not in school, we're still thinking about it, worrying about it, and comparing ourselves to others who seem to have it all figured out. This isn't just stressful; it's damaging to our mental health.

And then there's the issue of social media itself. These platforms are designed to keep us engaged for as long as possible. The more time we spend on them, the more ads we see, and the more money the platforms make. But this comes at a cost. The constant need to be online, to check what's happening, to see if we're getting enough likes, is draining. It's not just that we're wasting time; it's that we're sacrificing our mental health for something that doesn't even make us happy.

We must start rethinking how we use social media and approach mental health. This isn't just about taking a break from Instagram or spending less time online, although that can help. It's about changing the way we think about ourselves and our worth. It's about realizing that our value isn't determined by how many likes we get or how perfect our lives look on social media. It's about understanding that everyone struggles, that no one's life is as perfect as it seems online, and that it's okay to be imperfect.

But we can't do this alone. Schools, parents, and communities need to step up and start supporting mental health in real, meaningful ways. This means having honest conversations about the pressures we're facing, providing resources for those who are struggling, and creating environments where it's okay to talk about mental health without fear of judgment. It also means rethinking how we approach education and work so that we're not constantly pushing ourselves to the brink in pursuit of success.

The mental health crisis we're facing is a sign that something needs to change. As part of the anxious generation, we can make that change. By recognizing the impact of social media and the digital world on our mental health and by demanding better support from the systems around us, we can start to create a world where mental well-being is a priority, not an afterthought. It won't be easy, but if we work together, we can build a future where technology enhances our lives instead of making them more difficult. It's time to take control of our mental health and create a society that values us for who we are, not just for how we appear online.

IMPACT ON FAMILIES

In the past, when a child in a family struggled with anxiety, it was typically a private matter. Families would deal with it quietly, hoping the anxiety would pass on its own or eventually seeking help when it became clear it wouldn't. But the landscape has changed drastically in recent years. Now, anxiety in children is more visible, more diagnosed, and more talked about. It's almost impossible to ignore the rising numbers of kids dealing with anxiety disorders. You see it everywhere—kids as young as preschool age showing signs of stress and anxiety, and parents scrambling to find the best ways to help their children cope.

Today, it's not just about waiting to see if a child will grow out of their anxiety. Parents are more proactive than ever, investing time, energy, and money into getting their children the help they need. But this eagerness to intervene isn't just because the problems are worsening. Parents also feel immense pressure to do everything possible for their children. The fear of failing their child, of not giving them the best of what's out there, drives parents to push harder, spend more, and worry more.

The impact of a child's anxiety reaches far beyond the child alone. It touches every corner of family life. Parents who once felt confident in their parenting now question every decision. They watch their child closely, analyzing every behavior and every mood swing, trying to decipher if it's just a bad day or something more serious.

The constant monitoring and worrying become a full-time job, adding to the already heavy load that comes with parenting.

The financial burden is another weight that many families carry. Therapy sessions, medications, and various forms of intervention are costly, and the costs add up quickly. Families navigate a maze of healthcare options and insurance policies and sometimes even go out of pocket to ensure their child gets the best care. However, financial strain is just one part of the equation. The emotional toll can be even greater. Parents often feel a mix of frustration, helplessness, and guilt. They wonder if they're doing enough or making the right choices for their child. This emotional rollercoaster can be exhausting, leaving parents drained yet still pushing forward because of their deep love for their children.

In this journey, many parents turn to support groups, therapists, and other families going through similar experiences. There's a sense of comfort in knowing they're not alone and that others face the same challenges. Sharing stories, advice, and even just venting can be a lifeline, helping parents feel understood and supported.

As awareness of childhood anxiety grows, society is slowly starting to respond. Schools are beginning to recognize the importance of emotional well-being, integrating programs that teach kids coping mechanisms from an early age. Mental health professionals work more closely with parents and educators, creating strategies tailored to each child's needs. This collaborative approach gives families more tools to help their children, and more importantly, it fosters a sense of hope. Families are finding that they're not just surviving this challenge but learning to navigate it with resilience and strength.

But it's important to remember that anxiety isn't always a crisis. It's a natural part of the human experience, a response that can sometimes be protective. For instance, a young child who feels no fear might run into a busy street without understanding the danger or approach a snarling dog without caution. Anxiety, in these cases, is a helpful tool, teaching children to be cautious in situations that could harm them.

Experts in psychology, like Hughes, have pointed out that anxiety has a place in healthy development. Even children who are considered well-adjusted and come from supportive families can experience significant levels of stress. This doesn't mean something is wrong; it's just part of growing up in a world that can be overwhelming and complex.

The modern world, with its rapid changes and constant connectivity, can amplify these feelings of anxiety. Today's children are growing up in an environment vastly different from the one their parents knew. The pressure to keep up, be connected, and succeed in a fast-paced world can feel too much. But this anxiety also reflects something deeper—the vulnerability that is inherent in being human. It's a reminder that while we've made incredible advancements in technology and communication, we're still grappling with the same basic emotions and challenges that have always been part of life.

For families, understanding this can be both a challenge and a comfort. It's a challenge because it means accepting that anxiety might always be part of their child's life in some way. But it's also a comfort because it puts their child's experience into a broader context. It's not just about what's happening in their home—it's about what's happening in the world. Knowing this can help families find the strength to keep going, supporting their child, and hoping for a brighter, more balanced future.

In the end, the goal isn't to eliminate anxiety but to help children learn how to manage it in a way that allows them to lead happy, fulfilling lives. It's about balancing protecting them from the world's dangers and giving them the tools to face them confidently. It's about helping them grow into adults who can navigate the complexities of life with resilience and grace. And for parents, it's about finding peace in the knowledge that they're doing everything possible to help their child thrive.

SOCIETAL IMPLICATIONS

In recent years, the term "anxious generation" has become more prevalent, with media and mental health experts increasingly sounding the alarm about the surging levels of anxiety among young people. It's hard to ignore the data pointing to a significant rise in anxiety disorders across modern societies. In the United States, for example, nearly half of college students reported feeling "overwhelming anxiety" within the past year, according to the American College Health Association's Fall 2018 National College Health Assessment Report. The United Kingdom is experiencing a similar crisis, with the number of students seeking counseling for anxiety disorders increasing by a staggering 155 percent between 2009 and 2019, as revealed by the Cambridge project at the University of Cambridge.

The rise in anxiety isn't just about numbers on a page—it's a call to action. We need to address this growing mental health crisis with comprehensive and accessible resources. Untreated anxiety doesn't just go away; it festers and grows, affecting every aspect of a young person's life and, by extension, society as a whole.

Through research for her University of Winchester Ph.D. work, one expert delved into how social media contributes to this anxiety epidemic among young people. The critical period for developing clinical levels of anxiety and mood-related disorders typically spans from late childhood through the mid-20s. This vulnerability is further exacerbated by events and situations beyond their control, making timely support during these stages crucial for preventing long-term mental health issues.

Labeling is another significant factor. Young people, who are still developing their sense of self, can quickly internalize an anxious identity. This process is often accelerated by the pressure to conform to societal expectations and commercial marketing targeting their insecurities. The rapid maturation process can make adopting and internalizing an anxious identity feel almost inevitable. When young people see their peers achieving certain milestones or living seemingly perfect lives online, they feel pressured to measure up, intensifying their anxiety.

The challenges facing today's youth are multifaceted and complex. Social media platforms expose them to immense pressure, from maintaining a flawless online presence to fearing they're missing out on experiences their peers are having. Academic stress, societal expectations, and the turbulent transition to adulthood only add to the burden. These pressures make it difficult for young people to enjoy their youth and often leave them feeling overwhelmed and anxious.

Comprehensive support systems tailored to young people's unique needs are essential to combat these issues. This includes offering timely welfare assistance during critical developmental stages to reduce the risk of debilitating mental disorders significantly. Addressing the issue of labeling is also crucial. Young people need guidance to develop a healthy sense of self and avoid internalizing an anxious identity. By challenging the influence of commercial marketing and promoting messages of positivity and self-acceptance, we can help young people build resilience and self-assurance.

Society must acknowledge and actively address these challenges, fostering an environment that supports the holistic well-being of young individuals. We must instill a culture of empathy, understanding, and personal growth, empowering the younger generation to embrace their individuality and navigate uncertainties with resilience.

Take, for instance, the story of Emily, a high school student overwhelmed by the pressure to maintain high grades and a perfect social media presence. The constant comparisons with her peers left her feeling inadequate and anxious. Her parents, noticing her distress, sought help from a mental health professional who specialized in adolescent anxiety. Through therapy, Emily learned coping mechanisms and gradually built a healthier relationship with social media. She focused more on her passions and less on what others thought of her. Emily's journey highlights the importance of timely intervention and its positive impact on a young person's mental health.

The pressure to conform and manage anxieties can be overwhelming for young people, hindering their ability to enjoy the carefree moments of youth. By actively fostering an environment that supports their well-being, we can help them embrace their individuality and lead fulfilling lives free from anxiety. It's about creating a society where young people feel valued for who they are, not just how they measure up to others. This shift requires a collective effort, from parents and educators to policymakers and mental health professionals, to ensure that the next generation grows up resilient, confident, and capable of navigating the complexities of modern life.

In conclusion, the rise of anxiety among young people is a societal issue that demands urgent attention. By providing comprehensive support systems, addressing the root causes of stress, and promoting a culture of empathy and understanding, we can help the anxious generation thrive. It's time to move beyond just recognizing the problem and start implementing solutions that will make a real difference in the lives of young people today and in the future.

CULTURAL ANALYSIS OF SOCIETAL RESPONSES

Cultural narratives around anxiety have shifted dramatically in recent years. Today, anxiety is often viewed as a marker of modernity, something that reflects an individual's engagement with the world's complexities. Unlike traditional depression, which might be seen as more isolating and passive, anxiety is sometimes portrayed as a sign of heightened sensitivity, an edgy and authentic reaction to the pressures of contemporary life. It's almost as if, in some circles, anxiety has become a badge of honor—a way to signal that one is tuned in, aware, and deeply invested in the societal and global issues that define our times.

But this perspective has its complications. On one hand, anxiety is increasingly recognized as a legitimate response to the cultural and social pressures that so many of us face. It's seen as a logical, even predictable, reaction to a world that demands constant productivity, adaptability, and self-presentation. In this sense, anxiety is a social currency that reflects our values and participation in the social fabric. It speaks to our responsibility, awareness of societal issues, and engagement with the challenges of modern life.

On the other hand, the normalization of anxiety raises questions about the cultural expectations we place on ourselves and each other. As anxiety becomes more deeply embedded in our shared experiences and social norms, it starts to reflect the fragmentation and transformation of contemporary culture. We live in a time of rapid change and uncertainty, where the lines between personal space and social obligation are increasingly blurred. Anxiety, then, becomes a mirror, reflecting not just our struggles but also the broader societal dynamics at play.

Thinkers like Arendt and Sartre have explored how cultural expectations about freedom, both social and individual, intersect with our need to be integrated into society. This equation includes globalization, social learning, and the relentless push for self-optimization. In today's world, pharmaceutical companies play a significant role in shaping our attitudes toward mental health, promising solutions that are often more about managing symptoms than addressing root causes. Social media, too, contributes to this landscape, turning anxiety into a status contest where people measure their worth against the curated lives of others.

The challenge for us, as a society, is to navigate these complexities with care. We need to manage our expectations, recognize the fine line between help and harm, and seek out alternatives that prevent anxiety from spiraling into something more destructive. Religion and spirituality, whether institutional or not, have long provided a framework for coping with life's challenges. They offer community, structure, and a sense of purpose that can be grounded in an otherwise chaotic world. However, even these traditional supports are not always enough.

For many people, especially teenagers and young adults, the tools for coping with anxiety are not as straightforward. Coping skills and resilience training are valuable, but they don't always address the deeper issues that contribute to anxiety. There's a growing recognition that some ways society expects us to cope—through medication, therapy, or self-help strategies—are not one-size-fits-all solutions. What works for one person may not work for another, and there are no guarantees that any given approach will lead to lasting improvement.

This reality forces us to confront the limitations of our societal responses to anxiety. We cannot expect society to eliminate the responsibility of decision-making or to provide a guaranteed path to mental well-being. Mental illness, particularly anxiety, can sometimes serve as an avoidance strategy, a way to shield oneself from the discomfort of authenticity and self-creation. But this avoidance comes at a cost, inhibiting personal growth and the development of a true sense of self.

As a society, we need to evaluate the structures we've put in place to address anxiety and other mental health issues. Institutions should be held accountable for providing clear evaluations of the pros and cons of various treatments and interventions. We must also recognize that stress and coping are deeply intertwined with the larger dramas of contemporary life, resonating with individual conflicts and the broader social context.

In many ways, society acts as a nursemaid, guiding us through the complexities of modern life. But the connections between public discourse, anxiety, depression, and the development of our brains and minds are intricate and multifaceted. Every thought, every action, every decision we make is both a personal and a political act. The responsibilities of care—self-care and care for others—are deeply woven into the fabric of our society.

Anxiety, then, is not just a personal experience; it's a reflection of the broader social and political landscape. It's a symptom of a world in flux, where the pressures of modern life are both a burden and a call to action. As we grapple with the realities of anxiety, we must remember that it is both a personal responsibility and a shared, collective experience. How we respond to it—individually and as a society—will shape the future of our mental health and the kind of world we want to live in.

SELF-REFLECTION QUESTIONS

Personal Usage: Reflect on your use of digital technology within your family. How much time do you spend on daily devices for work, socializing, entertainment, and other purposes?

_____

_____

_____

_____

_____

_____

Quality of Interactions: Evaluate the quality of interactions with your family members before and after the introduction of digital technology. How has the frequency and depth of communication changed?

_____

_____

_____

_____

_____

_____

_____

Impact on Relationships: Consider how digital technology has influenced your relationships with family members. Have you noticed closeness, trust, or understanding changes due to digital interactions?

_____

_____

_____

_____

Balancing Screen Time: Can you balance digital device usage and face-to-face interactions with family members? How do you manage this balance?

_____

_____

_____

_____

Parenting Challenges: If you are a parent, reflect on the challenges of managing your children's screen time. How do you set boundaries and rules around technology use within your family?

_____

_____

_____

_____

Emotional Impact: How does digital technology affect your emotional well-being within the family context? Do you ever feel disconnected or overwhelmed by digital interactions?

_____

_____

_____

_____

_____

Cultural and Social Influences: Consider any cultural or societal norms that influence your family's approach to digital technology. How do these norms shape your family's dynamics and interactions?

_____

_____

_____

_____

_____

Exercise:

Discuss with peers or family members how digital technology has impacted your family dynamics using the following prompts:

Opening Discussion: Start by asking how each person feels about the role of digital technology in family life. Encourage everyone to share their perspectives and experiences.

Sharing Experiences: Share specific examples of how digital technology has affected daily routines, communication patterns, and relationships within your family.

Identifying Challenges: Identify common challenges or concerns arising from using digital technology within your family. Discuss how these challenges impact family dynamics and well-being.

Setting Goals: Brainstorm how to address these challenges together—set goals for reducing screen time, improving communication, or fostering more meaningful offline interactions.

Creating Solutions: Collaboratively develop strategies to enhance family bonding and reduce the negative impact of digital technology. Consider implementing technology-free zones or designated times for family activities.

Reflecting on Benefits: Discuss any positive aspects of digital technology within your family, such as educational resources, staying connected with distant relatives, or opportunities for creative expression.

CHAPTER SIX
DIAGNOSING COLLECTIVE ACTION PROBLEMS

"Addressing collective action problems requires a shared understanding of the challenges we face and a collaborative effort towards sustainable solutions." -
Elinor Ostrom

D iagnosing collective action problems in the context of today's anxious generation is not just a theoretical exercise—it's a vital exploration of how our society, driven by digital interactions and social media, grapples with challenges that affect not only individuals but entire groups. The way we, as a society, respond to these challenges can profoundly impact our collective well-being, particularly for teenagers who are navigating a world that feels increasingly fragmented and uncertain.

Despite his struggles with paranoid schizophrenia, John Nash made groundbreaking contributions to game theory. This framework can help us understand how individuals and groups make decisions that impact the broader society. Nash's insights into the dynamics of cooperation and competition are especially relevant today as we try to make sense of the anxieties and collective challenges facing the younger generation.

Imagine a group of teenagers, each grappling with their insecurities and fears, but all interconnected through social media. They're all part of the same online communities, sharing snippets of their lives, thoughts, and emotions. But instead of fostering a sense of togetherness, these platforms often amplify feelings of isolation and competition. Each teen sees the carefully curated lives of others, which triggers a collective anxiety—a sense that they're not measuring up or falling behind in some unspoken race.

This scenario is a modern manifestation of the collective action problems Nash's theories help us understand. In game theory, individuals must make decisions that balance their interests with the groups'. But what happens when the "game" is life itself, played out in the digital arena? Each decision to post a photo, comment, or like might seem trivial, but it contributes to a larger pattern of behavior that can either uplift or drag down the group's mental health.

For example, take the phenomenon of "FOMO" (fear of missing out). It's a classic collective action problem in the digital age. Teenagers see their friends posting about a party or a gathering they weren't invited to, and they feel anxious. This anxiety isn't just about missing the event; it's about feeling excluded, about not being part of the group. The more teens experience FOMO, the more they might engage in behaviors that exacerbate the problem—posting their photos to show they're having fun, even if they're not, or constantly checking their phones to stay in the loop. These behaviors, in turn, fuel the cycle of anxiety for everyone else in the group.

Nash's work teaches us that short-term, self-interested decisions can lead to negative outcomes for the entire group in such scenarios. If each teenager is focused solely on presenting the best version of their life online, they contribute to a collective environment where anxiety and competition thrive. In this context, the "Nash equilibrium" is a state where everyone is making choices based on what they think others will do, but no one is truly happy or fulfilled. The equilibrium, while stable, is deeply unsatisfying.

We need to rethink how we approach collective action in the digital age to break out of this cycle. One possible solution is fostering a culture of authenticity and support, where teens are encouraged to share their highlights and struggles. When one teen opens up about feeling anxious or overwhelmed, it can create a ripple effect, encouraging others to do the same. This shift can lead to a new equilibrium where the group's well-being is prioritized over individual appearances.

Another important factor is the role of emotions in shaping collective behavior. Nash's theories often focus on rational decision-making, but emotions play a critical role in the real world. Fear, insecurity, and the desire for acceptance are powerful drivers of behavior for teenagers. Understanding this can help us develop better strategies for addressing collective action problems.

For instance, imagine a school implementing a program that teaches students about the emotional impact of social media. By helping teens recognize how their online behavior affects not only their mental health but also the mental health of their peers, the program could encourage more thoughtful and supportive interactions. This kind of initiative could help shift the group's collective behavior, reducing the prevalence of anxiety and fostering a healthier online environment.

The pressures of modern life, particularly for teenagers, often lead to behaviors that prioritize short-term relief over long-term well-being. This might mean seeking validation through likes and comments rather than meaningful connections in the digital age. Society's challenge is to create structures and support systems that encourage more sustainable, fulfilling ways of interacting.

In the context of Nash's work, we can see that the solutions to these collective action problems aren't easy. They require a deep understanding of the dynamics and willingness to engage with the emotional and psychological factors that drive behavior. But suppose we can harness the insights from game theory and apply them to the challenges of the digital age. In that case, we might find a way to help the anxious generation navigate their world more confidently and less fearfully.

In this way, Nash's legacy extends far beyond mathematics and economics. His theories provide us with tools to understand and address the complex social dynamics shaping teenagers' lives today. By diagnosing these collective action problems and working towards solutions, we can create a society that supports the mental health and well-being of all its members, particularly those most vulnerable to modern life's pressures..

IDENTIFYING THE ROOT CAUSES

In the age we live in, anxiety seems to have woven itself into the very fabric of our daily existence. It's as if everywhere we turn, there's something else to worry about or stress over. Statistics tell part of the story: nearly 18% of American adults are diagnosed with an anxiety disorder, and almost 40% experience excessive anxiety regularly. But these numbers are more than just data points—they reflect a deep-seated issue brewing in our society for decades.

Looking back, we can see that anxiety isn't a new phenomenon. Even in the 1950s, there were signs that something was amiss. Surveys from as far back as 1953 reveal that college students were already grappling with anxiety, a trend that has only intensified over the years. By 1955, the term "An Age of Anxiety" had already entered popular culture, signaling a collective recognition that something was wrong. Today, this sense of unease has only grown, becoming almost a defining feature of modern life.

To understand why anxiety is so prevalent today, we need to look at the broader cultural and societal factors at play. One of the root causes is the relentless pressure that modern life imposes on us. Whether it's the pressure to succeed at work, to maintain a certain social status, or to keep up with the constant barrage of information and expectations, it feels like we're always on edge. There's a sense that we need to be constantly doing more, achieving more, and being more—often at the expense of our mental health.

Media and cultural narratives play a significant role in amplifying this anxiety. How we consume news, entertainment, and even social media creates a heightened sense of urgency and stress. We're bombarded with images and stories that remind us of everything we should be worried about, from global crises to personal insecurities. It's no wonder that so many of us feel overwhelmed.

Then there's the issue of stimulants like caffeine, which are deeply embedded in our daily routines. Coffee, energy drinks, and other caffeinated products are often considered necessary tools to get through the day, especially in a society that values productivity above all else. But while caffeine can give us a quick boost, it also exacerbates anxiety symptoms, creating a vicious cycle where we're constantly trying to keep up with the demands of life while our bodies and minds are being pushed to the limit.

For young people, particularly teenagers, the situation is even more complex. They're growing up in a world where the expectations are sky-high, and the pressure to conform is intense. Social media, while offering a platform for connection, also constantly reminds them of what they lack—whether it's popularity, success, or physical appearance. This constant comparison can be devastating for their self-esteem and mental health, leading to heightened levels of anxiety. The roots of this anxiety can be traced back to the way our society is structured. We live in a world that prioritizes achievement and success over well-being. From a young age, we're taught that our worth is measured by our accomplishments—grades in school, achievements in sports, and success in our careers. This focus on external validation creates a pervasive sense of inadequacy as if we're never quite good enough. It's this underlying feeling of insufficiency that drives much of the anxiety we see today.

In addition to societal pressures, there's also the role of the economy. The economic landscape has shifted dramatically over the past few decades, with increasing job insecurity, rising living costs, and a widening gap between the rich and the poor. These economic pressures add another layer of stress to an already anxious population. For many, the fear of being unable to make ends meet or falling behind financially is a constant source of worry.

So, what can be done to address this pervasive anxiety? First, we must recognize that this is a collective issue, not just an individual one. It's not enough to tell people to "just relax" or "take a break." We must create a society that values mental health and well-being as much as success and productivity. This means rethinking our cultural narratives, work environments, and even our educational systems to emphasize balance and mental health more.

For teenagers and young adults, this might involve creating more supportive online and offline environments. Schools can play a critical role by incorporating mental health education into their curricula and providing resources for struggling students. Social media platforms, too, are responsible for creating spaces that are less about competition and comparison and more about genuine connection and support.

On an individual level, it's important to find ways to manage anxiety that work for us. This might involve cutting back on caffeine, setting boundaries with social media, or finding healthy outlets for stress, like exercise or creative activities. But more than anything, it's about recognizing that we don't have to do it all or be it all. Sometimes, just being enough is exactly what we need.

In conclusion, the root causes of our current anxiety epidemic are deeply intertwined with our society's structures and values. To truly address this issue, we need to take a holistic approach, looking at everything from cultural narratives to economic pressures. Only by understanding and addressing these underlying causes can we hope to create a world where anxiety isn't the norm but the exception.

SELF-REFLECTION QUESTIONS

How has digital technology impacted your daily life and interactions with others in your community?

_____

_____

_____

Are you aware of the digital dependency issues in your local community? How do you perceive its effects on individuals and families?

_____

_____

_____

_____

What role do you believe you play in addressing digital dependency within your community?

_____

_____

_____

_____

How engaged do you feel with your local community in discussing and addressing issues related to digital technology use?

_____

_____

_____

_____

_____

What values are essential to uphold when considering solutions to digital dependency? How do these align with community values?

_____

_____

_____

_____

_____

What kind of community do you envision regarding healthy digital interactions and balanced screen-time practices?

_____

_____

_____

_____

_____

Exercise:

Brainstorming Community-Based Solutions to Address Digital Dependency

Goals:

- Initiate discussions involving all community stakeholders to create realistic action plans.

- Develop a collective strategy to promote healthy interactions with digital technologies.

- Formulate future community action plans to enhance humanity through responsible digital use.

Exercise Steps:

What specific digital dependency issues are prevalent in our community?

_____

_____

_____

Who are the key stakeholders in our community who should be involved in addressing these issues?

_____

_____

_____

How can we develop actionable steps to promote healthy digital habits collaboratively?

_____

_____

_____

What resources (e.g., education programs, community events) are needed to support these initiatives?

_____

_____

_____

How will we evaluate the effectiveness of our actions? How can community feedback shape future strategies?

_____

_____

_____

Discussion Starters:

- How can we encourage families to establish screen-time guidelines that promote balance and well-being?
- What role can schools play in educating students and parents about responsible digital use?
- How can local businesses and organizations support initiatives to reduce digital dependency among youth?

Chapter Note

_____

_____

_____

_____

_____

_____

_____

_____

_____

_____

_____

_____

_____

_____

_____

_____

_____

_____

_____

_____

_____

_____

_____

_____

CHAPTER SEVEN
PROPOSING SOLUTIONS

"Innovative solutions emerge when we combine insights from psychology, technology, and social policy to address the complex challenges of digital dependency." –
Angela Duckworth

We live in a world where the relentless march of industrialization and globalization has reshaped our economies and the fabric of our emotional lives. The rapid expansion of psychiatry, while beneficial in many respects, has also led to an increasing number of individuals—especially teenagers—who find themselves struggling with emotional and psychological challenges. These challenges are often magnified by the digital environments in which they are immersed, where the pressure to perform, conform, and succeed is relentless.

For teenagers today, anxiety isn't just an individual issue—it's a collective one. The pressures they face are not isolated incidents but part of a broader societal pattern. In a culture that prizes achievement and visibility, where social media amplifies every success and failure, it's no wonder that many young people find themselves overwhelmed. The inability to adapt to this constant pressure isn't just a personal failing—it's a reflection of a society that has yet to find a balance between progress and well-being.

But the solution isn't as simple as expanding access to psychiatric services or increasing the prescription of medications. While these interventions can be helpful, they often address the symptoms rather than the root causes of anxiety. To truly support this generation, we need to step back and examine the broader cultural forces at play.

One of the most significant issues we face is the way we understand and label anxiety. In the Western world, there's a tendency to view anxiety as something that needs to be fixed, something that stands in the way of a happy, successful life. This perspective can lead to an over-reliance on medication as a quick fix rather than encouraging young people to develop the resilience needed to navigate life's challenges.

Yet, anxiety is not always a disorder to be eradicated. It can also be a signal—a reflection of the real pressures and uncertainties that define modern life. For teenagers, the challenge is often not in eliminating anxiety but in learning how to live with it, how to interpret it, and how to respond to it in a way that promotes growth rather than paralysis.

Consider, for example, the impact of social media. These platforms were designed to connect us, but they often isolate us, creating a culture of comparison that fuels insecurity and self-doubt. Teenagers, who are still developing their sense of self, are particularly vulnerable to this. They are constantly bombarded with images of others' curated lives, leading them to question their worth and achievements. The result is a pervasive sense of inadequacy that can quickly spiral into anxiety.

The challenge for us, then, is to create online and offline environments that help young people navigate these pressures. This means teaching them to recognize the difference between healthy, productive anxiety and the kind that can overwhelm them. It also means fostering a culture that values authenticity over perfection and encourages young people to share their real experiences, not just their highlights.

But changing the culture isn't enough. We also need to address the underlying societal structures that contribute to this anxiety. This includes rethinking our educational systems, which often place undue stress on achievement and success at the expense of well-being. It means challenging the economic pressures that drive so many young people to feel that they must constantly be on the move, continually striving for more.

In this context, the role of families, schools, and communities becomes crucial. We must create support systems that help young people build their resilience to thrive in this environment. This might involve integrating mental health education into school curricula, providing resources for parents, and creating spaces where teenagers can talk about their experiences without fear of judgment.

Ultimately, the goal is not to eliminate anxiety but to help young people develop the tools they need to manage it. This means recognizing that anxiety is often a natural response to the world we live in and that the key to managing it lies not in avoidance but in engagement. By helping teenagers understand and navigate their anxiety, we can empower them to face the challenges of modern life with confidence and resilience.

In doing so, we support their well-being and contribute to a healthier, more balanced society—one where the pressures of modern life are acknowledged and addressed rather than medicated away, one where young people are given the tools they need to thrive, not just survive. This way, we can ensure that the anxious generation becomes resilient, resourceful, and ready to take on the world.

STEPS FOR PARENTS OF TEENS AND YOUNG ADULTS

Parenting in today's digital age is like walking a tightrope, especially for teenagers. On one side, you want to provide the support they need to navigate their anxieties and challenges. Conversely, you need to give them the space to grow, make mistakes, and learn to handle life's pressures independently. Striking this balance is not easy, but it's essential for helping teens become resilient and capable adults.

One of the most important tools in a parent's toolkit is what some call "compassionate detachment." This means offering your child wisdom, love, and support without smothering them with worry. It's a delicate dance. Your teenager might mistake your concern for overbearing anxiety, which can lead them to shut down or push you away. It can backfire when you hover too closely, constantly looking for signs that something might be wrong. Teens need to know you're there for them, but they also need the freedom to figure things out independently.

Imagine your teenager as a ship setting sail. Your role as a parent is to be the lighthouse, providing guidance and light but not steering the boat. They need to navigate the waters, learning to handle the storms that come their way. Your supportive presence and ability to step back and allow them to chart their course is crucial. This doesn't mean ignoring warning signs or abandoning your role as a parent. It means trusting in their ability to learn from their experiences, even when those experiences include anxiety and uncertainty.

Anxiety is a complex emotion, and understanding it can be half the battle. For teenagers who are already dealing with the emotional rollercoaster of adolescence, anxiety can be particularly confusing and overwhelming. As a parent, one of the best things you can do is help them understand what anxiety is and how it works. This doesn't mean giving them a psychology lecture but having open, honest conversations about their feelings.

Explain that anxiety is a normal part of life and that everyone experiences it in some form. It's the body's way of responding to stress, but it doesn't have to control their life. By demystifying anxiety, you take away some of its power. Share practical strategies that they can use when anxiety starts to take over—whether it's deep breathing, mindfulness techniques, or simply taking a walk to clear their head. The goal is to equip them with tools they can use independently, reinforcing the idea that they have the power to manage their anxiety.

In today's world, where teenagers are constantly bombarded by the pressures of social media and the unrealistic standards it promotes, helping them build a toolkit of coping mechanisms is more important than ever. It's not just about surviving high school; it's about preparing them for a life where they can navigate challenges with confidence and resilience.

No one should have to face anxiety alone, and this is especially true for teenagers. Beyond the immediate family, having a network of supportive mentors can make a world of difference. These could be relatives, teachers, coaches, or even friends who positively influence your child. These figures can provide perspective, share their own experiences, and offer advice that might resonate differently than it does coming from a parent.

Sometimes, teens must hear from someone outside the family to let the message sink in. These mentors can play a crucial role in helping them manage anxiety by offering different viewpoints and strategies. By surrounding your child with a diverse group of caring individuals, you give them access to various coping strategies and emotional support systems to help them find what works best for them.

In an age where online interactions often replace face-to-face connections, fostering real-world relationships becomes even more critical. Encourage your teenager to seek out these mentors and value their support network. It's one of the best ways to help them build resilience and a sense of security.

Communication is the foundation of any strong relationship, and this is especially true when it comes to parenting teenagers. When your teen comes to you with a problem or concern, resist the urge to jump in with advice or solutions. Instead, focus on listening to what they have to say. Ask open-ended questions, encouraging them to share their feelings and thoughts.

This approach helps you understand what your teenager is going through and shows them that you respect their opinions and value their perspective. It creates a safe space where they feel comfortable opening up, knowing they won't be met with immediate judgment or criticism.

For many teenagers in the digital age, where so much of their communication happens online, having these real, in-person conversations can be incredibly grounding. It helps them feel seen and heard in an overwhelming and isolating world.

By prioritizing active listening over lecturing, you're also modeling a valuable skill they can carry into their relationships. You're teaching them that effective communication is a two-way street and that sometimes, the best support you can offer is simply being there to listen.

Parenting in the digital age, especially with the rise of the "anxious generation," requires a thoughtful and balanced approach. It's about providing guidance and independence, equipping your teenager with the tools they need to manage their anxiety, and fostering a strong support network they can rely on.

Your goal as a parent is to help your teenager become a confident, resilient adult who can face life's challenges with courage and grace. By practicing compassionate detachment, educating and empowering them, building a strong support network, and prioritizing listening over lecturing, you're setting them up for success—not just in managing anxiety but all aspects of their life.

STRATEGIES FOR SCHOOLS AND EDUCATIONAL INSTITUTIONS

Addressing anxiety within our educational systems is not just a necessity but a moral imperative. The stress that many students experience in school is not a transient phase; if left unaddressed, it's often a harbinger of long-term mental health challenges. Schools are not just places for academic learning—they are environments where young people should feel supported, understood, and equipped with the skills they need to navigate the complexities of life.

The pressures that students face today are multifaceted. Exams, interviews, and presentations are high-stakes events that can trigger significant anxiety. The fear of failure, the pressure to meet expectations, and the uncertainty of outcomes create a breeding ground for stress. These experiences can leave lasting scars, fostering a sense of inadequacy and helplessness that can persist into adulthood.

But the roots of this anxiety often run deeper than the immediate pressures of schoolwork. Many students need help with unrealistic time constraints, diverse performance expectations that feel ever-changing, and rigid subject limitations that stifle their curiosity and passion. The school environment can sometimes exacerbate these issues, with inflexible structures that don't accommodate students' diverse needs and learning styles. When parents, too, are stretched thin—unable to provide the necessary emotional support due to their time pressures or lack of resources—students can feel isolated in their struggles, compounding their anxiety.

So, what can schools and educational institutions do to create a more supportive environment that addresses these issues head-on?

1. Reducing Time Pressure and Managing Expectations

One of the most effective strategies is reducing the time pressure that students and their families face. Schools can start by re-evaluating the amount of homework assigned, ensuring it is reasonable and aligned with students' capacities. Homework should reinforce learning, not become a source of stress that eats into family time and personal well-being. Flexible deadlines and the ability to negotiate due dates for significant assignments can also help students manage their workload more effectively.

In addition to managing time pressures, schools should aim to set realistic and attainable student expectations. Rather than pushing for perfection, educators should encourage a growth mindset—where effort, improvement, and learning from mistakes are valued over simply getting high grades. This shift in focus can alleviate some anxiety associated with academic performance and help students build resilience.

2. Gradual Introduction of New Concepts and Experiences

Students today are bombarded with information at a rapid pace. While exposure to new ideas and experiences is essential for learning, it can also be overwhelming. Schools should consider pacing the introduction of new material, allowing students time to digest and process what they've learned before moving on to the next topic. This approach helps reduce cognitive overload and makes learning more manageable.

Moreover, teachers can implement "scaffolded" learning techniques, where new concepts are built on prior knowledge incrementally. This reinforces understanding and boosts confidence as students realize they can master complex subjects step by step.

3. Implementing Holistic Educational Models

Innovative educational models, like Lomilo's psychological school model, can provide a more holistic approach to education. This model integrates different subjects and carefully plans the day's curriculum to consider students' psychological and emotional well-being. By balancing academic rigor with psychological support, schools can create an environment where students feel more secure and less anxious.

This might mean creating a school schedule that alternates between challenging subjects and more relaxed, creative classes. It could also involve integrating mindfulness practices or "well-being breaks" throughout the day, allowing students to recharge and refocus.

4. Building a Supportive School Culture

A supportive school culture is essential for reducing anxiety. This starts with training teachers and staff to recognize the signs of stress and providing them with the tools to support students effectively. Schools can also establish peer support systems, where students are trained to assist their classmates. This peer-led approach can be particularly effective, as students may feel more comfortable talking to someone their age.

In addition to peer support, schools should offer accessible mental health resources, such as counseling services or well-being workshops. Regular check-ins with students can help identify struggling students and provide timely interventions.

5. Fostering Open Communication and Parental Involvement

Schools should encourage open communication between teachers, students, and parents. Regular parent-teacher conferences that focus on academic performance and the student's emotional and social development can provide a more comprehensive understanding of the child's needs. Schools can also offer workshops for parents, helping them develop the skills needed to support their child's mental health at home.

By involving parents in the conversation about anxiety and mental health, schools can create a more cohesive support system for students. When students see their teachers and parents working together, they are more likely to feel supported and understood.

6. Empirical Evaluation and Adaptation

Finally, schools need to commit to ongoing evaluation of these strategies. What works for one student body might not be as effective for another, and students' needs can change over time. Schools should collect data on the effectiveness of their interventions and be willing to adapt their approaches as necessary. This might involve regular surveys of students and parents, as well as consultations with mental health professionals.

By taking a proactive and flexible approach, schools can ensure that they are meeting the needs of their students in real time rather than relying on outdated methods.

In conclusion, addressing the issue of anxiety in schools requires a comprehensive, multifaceted approach. Schools can create environments where students feel supported and empowered by reducing time pressures, managing expectations, pacing the introduction of new material, implementing holistic educational models, building a supportive culture, fostering open communication, and committing to empirical evaluation. This is not just about improving academic performance—it's about ensuring that our children grow up to be healthy, resilient adults equipped to handle life's challenges.

RECOMMENDATIONS FOR TECH COMPANIES AND PLATFORMS

The ongoing debate about technology and social media's impact on mental health is not just a topic for academic discussion; it's a pressing issue that directly affects the lives of millions, particularly teenagers and young adults. As we navigate through this digital age, it's becoming increasingly clear that while technology offers tremendous benefits, it also carries risks that can contribute to anxiety and mental health struggles. For the "anxious generation," these issues are more than just theoretical—they are lived experiences that shape their day-to-day lives.

For tech companies and platforms, the challenge is not only to acknowledge these concerns but also to take meaningful steps to mitigate their products' negative impacts. This isn't about vilifying technology or placing blame on developers; rather, it's about creating a digital environment that promotes well-being and supports mental health. The following recommendations aim to guide tech companies in making their platforms safer and healthier spaces for users, particularly the younger demographic.

Develop Tools to Combat Over-Reliance and Addiction

One of the most significant issues with modern technology is its addictive nature. Social media platforms are designed to keep users engaged, often at the cost of their mental health. Features like endless scrolling, instant notifications, and algorithm-driven content recommendations can lead to over-reliance on these platforms, fostering anxiety and stress. Tech companies must take responsibility for these outcomes by developing tools that help users manage their usage better.

For instance, platforms could introduce more robust time management features that allow users to limit their daily use. These tools should be easily accessible and highly customizable, enabling users to tailor their experience to their needs. Additionally, providing users with detailed insights into their usage patterns can help them become more aware of how much time they spend online and how it affects their mental health. By giving users more control over their digital interactions, tech companies can help reduce the compulsive behaviors that often lead to anxiety.

Simplify Time Management and User Control

The complexity of managing digital time can be overwhelming, especially for younger users who may still need to gain the skills to self-regulate effectively. Tech companies can simplify these processes and offer clear, actionable suggestions for healthier usage to help users understand and control how they spend their time online.

This could include features like automated reminders to take breaks, suggestions for alternative activities based on usage patterns, or even personalized recommendations for digital detox periods. These tools should be user-friendly and align with individual preferences, allowing users to maintain a balanced and intentional relationship with technology.

Intensify Research on Technology's Impact on Mental Health

Understanding the full impact of technology on mental health requires more than anecdotal evidence; it demands rigorous, ongoing research. Tech companies are uniquely positioned to lead this research, given their vast access to user data. By investing in studies that explore the connections between technology use, anxiety, and overall mental health, companies can gain valuable insights into how their platforms affect users.

This comprehensive research should examine short-term and long-term effects across various demographics. It should also consider how technology is used, from social media to gaming. The findings from these studies can then inform product development, leading to features and services that better support mental well-being.

Expand and Invest in Online Mental Health Services

Given the widespread use of digital platforms, tech companies have a unique opportunity to provide accessible mental health support directly through their services. This could include partnerships with mental health organizations to offer therapy and counseling sessions online, providing users with easy access to professional help.

Moreover, these services should be tailored to meet the needs of the most vulnerable populations, including teenagers and young adults who are at higher risk of anxiety and depression. Personalized mental health resources, such as self-help tools, stress management techniques, and peer support networks, can make a significant difference in the lives of those struggling with mental health issues.

Promote Positive Online Environments

In addition to managing the direct impact of technology on mental health, tech companies must also focus on fostering positive online environments. Social media, in particular, can be a breeding ground for negativity, with cyberbullying, hate speech, and unrealistic comparisons contributing to increased anxiety among users.

Platforms can combat this by implementing stronger community guidelines, more effective moderation tools, and educational campaigns encouraging positive interactions. Creating a culture of kindness and support online can help reduce the stress and anxiety associated with social media use.

Encourage Mindful and Balanced Technology Use

Finally, tech companies should actively promote the concept of mindful technology use. This involves encouraging users to reflect on their engagement with technology and make conscious choices about their digital habits. Companies can integrate mindfulness prompts into their platforms, offer resources on digital well-being, and collaborate with mental health experts to develop content that guides users toward healthier usage patterns.

For example, apps could feature regular check-ins that ask users to assess their mood and reflect on their recent online activities. These prompts can serve as gentle reminders to take breaks, disconnect when needed, and prioritize offline interactions that contribute to their overall well-being.

As the world continues to evolve in this digital era, tech companies' responsibility goes beyond innovation and profit. It extends to the mental health and well-being of their users, especially the younger generation, who are most vulnerable to the pressures of the online world. By taking proactive steps to address the challenges associated with technology use, companies can help mitigate the anxiety that has become so prevalent among today's youth.

The "anxious generation" does not have to remain defined by their struggles. With thoughtful, responsible action from tech companies, we can build a digital landscape that supports mental health, fosters positive social interactions, and helps young people navigate the complexities of the modern world with confidence and resilience.

POLICIES FOR GOVERNMENTS AND PUBLIC HEALTH INITIATIVES

Governments hold a critical role in shaping the mental health landscape, especially as we confront the unique challenges of the digital age. The rapid growth of technology and social media has given rise to new forms of anxiety, particularly among teenagers, who are navigating a world that is vastly different from that of previous generations. To address the mental health crisis among this "anxious generation," governments must implement policies and public health initiatives that are both forward-thinking and rooted in the realities of the digital world.

One of the first steps governments can take is to recognize the unintended consequences of existing policies that may inadvertently contribute to rising anxiety levels. For example, the increasingly intolerant sociopolitical climate and the pressure of longer working hours don't just affect adults but trickle down to impact the younger generation as well. Teens are keenly aware of the stresses their parents and communities face, which, in turn, can heighten their anxieties. A more supportive and tolerant societal framework is crucial, as is the acknowledgment that the mental well-being of the population is a collective responsibility.

In this digital era, governments can leverage technology for good. By integrating digital tools and data analytics into public health strategies, they can develop more effective, evidence-based interventions tailored to the needs of today's youth. For instance, online platforms can provide mental health education and resources directly to teens, making help more accessible and less stigmatized. Governments could support the creation of apps that teach coping mechanisms and mindfulness practices and provide direct access to counseling services.

Moreover, educators play a pivotal role in this landscape. Governments must invest in training teachers and school staff to identify signs of anxiety early, both in students and in themselves. This means not only recognizing the visible signs but understanding the often subtle ways anxiety manifests in a digitally connected world—through social media use, online bullying, or the pressure to maintain a perfect online persona. Teachers should be equipped with the tools to support students, fostering a school environment that prioritizes mental health and academic achievement.

Public health statistics increasingly point to a mental health crisis that is outpacing the availability of professional help. To combat this, governments should prioritize preventative services that address mild anxiety before it escalates. This could involve community-based programs offering stress management workshops, peer support groups, and resilience-building activities. Schools could implement regular mental health check-ins, where students have a safe space to discuss their feelings without fear of judgment.

In addition to preventative measures, it's essential to tackle the broader societal pressures that contribute to teen anxiety. The relentless pursuit of success, as defined by grades, social status, or athletic achievement, often leaves young people feeling overwhelmed and inadequate. Governments can introduce social initiatives that promote a more balanced view of success, one that values emotional intelligence, creativity, and well-being as much as academic or professional accomplishments. This shift in cultural values would encourage teens to focus on their overall development rather than just their achievements.

Addressing systemic inequalities is another crucial component. Teens from underprivileged backgrounds often face additional stressors, such as financial instability or lack of access to resources, which exacerbate their mental health struggles. Public policies focusing on reducing these disparities—through improved access to education, healthcare, and social services—can significantly alleviate the burden on these young individuals. Investing in early childhood education, providing adequate support for families, and ensuring that all teens have access to the resources they need to succeed are fundamental steps toward creating a more equitable society.

Destigmatizing mental health, particularly severe anxiety, is equally important. In a digital age where perfection is often broadcasted across social media, teens who struggle with their mental health can feel isolated and ashamed. Governments should lead campaigns that normalize mental health challenges, encouraging open conversations and providing clear pathways to support. These campaigns could be integrated into school curriculums, public service announcements, and social media platforms, making mental health a topic as common and uncontroversial as physical health.

Furthermore, the creation of specialized mental health services for severe anxiety is necessary. These services should be accessible and tailored to the unique needs of teenagers, offering a range of options from psychosocial support to pharmacological treatments.

These services must be designed to be user-friendly, with input from teens to ensure they meet the actual needs of this demographic.

In conclusion, the role of governments in addressing the mental health of teenagers in the digital age is multifaceted. It requires a commitment to creating supportive environments, leveraging technology for positive outcomes, training educators, and implementing public health initiatives that are both preventative and responsive. By fostering a culture of understanding, empathy, and support, we can help the "anxious generation" navigate the complexities of modern life with resilience and confidence. The ultimate goal is to ensure that every young person has the opportunity to thrive in a world that values their mental health as much as their academic and social achievements.

SELF-REFLECTION QUESTIONS

Why do you feel passionate about advocating for policy changes in your community or school?

_____

_____

_____

_____

How familiar are you with the current policies and procedures that need changing?

_____

_____

_____

_____

What potential impacts could these policy changes have on students, families, teachers, and the broader community?

_____

_____

_____

_____

What skills or experiences do you bring to the advocacy process?

_____

_____

_____

How can you effectively contribute to achieving policy change?

_____

_____

_____

How do you plan to navigate challenges or setbacks in advocating for policy changes?

_____

_____

_____

What do you hope to learn or gain from this advocacy experience, personally and professionally?

_____

_____

_____

_____

How flexible can you adjust your advocacy strategies based on feedback and changing circumstances?

_____

_____

_____

_____

In what ways do you see yourself as a leader within your advocacy efforts? How will you leverage your influence to gain support for the proposed changes?

_____

_____

_____

_____

Reflect on when you faced a setback or challenge in advocating for something. How did you overcome it, and what did you learn from that experience?

_____

_____

_____

_____

What ethical considerations are important when advocating for policy changes? How will you ensure your advocacy is fair and inclusive?

_____

_____

_____

_____

Beyond this advocacy effort, what long-term impact do you hope to achieve in your community or school through policy advocacy?

_____

_____

_____

_____

How do you anticipate this experience of advocating for policy changes will contribute to your personal growth and development?

_____

_____

_____

_____

Exercise: Developing an Action Plan

Goals:

✓ Advocate for policy changes that improve the well-being and educational experience of students.

✓ Collaborate with stakeholders to build support and momentum for identified policy changes.

✓ Implement a strategic advocacy plan incorporating diverse tools and aligning with the six advocacy pointers.

Exercise Steps:

Identify Policy Areas: What specific policies or procedures in your community or school must be changed to better support students?

Assess Current Effectiveness: What aspects of these policies work well, and what aspects need improvement or change?

Advocacy Tools Selection:

Big Advocacy Tools: Identify larger-scale actions or strategies (e.g., community forums, petitions) that could create a significant impact.

Medium-Sized Advocacy Tools: Determine actions that involve moderate effort but could yield substantial results (e.g., meetings with school administrators, writing op-eds).

Small Advocacy Tools: Outline simple but effective actions (e.g., social media campaigns, creating informational flyers) to engage a broader audience.

Advocacy Pointers Integration: Incorporate the six advocacy pointers into your action plan, ensuring strategies are grounded in solid ide

as coalition-building and engagement with the policy-making process.

Community Engagement: How will you engage and mobilize students, parents, teachers, and community members to support your advocacy efforts?

Timeline and Evaluation: Develop a timeline for implementing your advocacy plan. How will you measure the success and impact of your advocacy efforts?

Discussion Starters:

How can we effectively communicate the need for policy changes to different stakeholders (e.g., parents and school board members)?

What partnerships or coalitions can we build to amplify our advocacy efforts and increase our influence?

How might we navigate potential resistance or opposition to proposed policy changes?

Chapter Note

_____

_____

_____

_____

_____

_____

_____

_____

_____

_____

_____

_____

_____

_____

_____

_____

_____

_____

_____

_____

_____

_____

_____

CHAPTER EIGHT
THE ROLE OF COMMUNITIES AND RITUALS

"Communities and rituals play a crucial role in fostering resilience and well-being in an increasingly digital world." –
Brené Brown

In the age of hyperconnectivity and outsourcing, we've drifted away from the value of localized rituals and the communal bonds that once provided a solid foundation for our mental and emotional well-being. In our pursuit of performance and success, we've lost touch with the cyclical nature of life, the kind that mirrors the turning of the seasons—a rhythm that used to guide our ancestors through the ebbs and flows of existence. The relentless push to perform consistently, day in and day out, without pause or reflection, has left us feeling disconnected and unfulfilled. This disconnection fuels the anxiety that permeates our lives, making us feel cheated by the very systems we rely on.

In many ways, our current societal structure encourages us to fight against natural cycles and deny the inevitability of change, whether it's changing seasons or the passage of time. This resistance only exacerbates our anxiety, driving us to seek out quick fixes rather than addressing the root causes. We often turn to necessity and fear when we consider treatments and interventions for anxiety, overlooking simpler, more cost-effective solutions that have been used for generations.

One of these overlooked solutions is the power of community and ritual. Humans thrive on connection, routine, and a sense of belonging—elements increasingly missing from our modern lives. Local customs and rituals once served as community touchstones, providing a sense of continuity and shared purpose. They helped individuals feel grounded and supported, offering a framework to navigate life's challenges. However, in today's fragmented and socially distanced world, these rituals have been pushed aside and replaced by a constant demand for productivity and self-reliance.

The result is a society where individuals feel isolated despite being more connected than ever through technology. We've lost the collective wisdom from participating in rituals that mark the passage of time and life's milestones. Without these rituals, we're left to navigate life's challenges alone, often feeling overwhelmed and unsupported. This isolation only deepens the anxiety that so many of us experience.

Communities are crucial in alleviating this anxiety by providing spaces where individuals can come together, share their experiences, and support one another. These communal spaces don't have to be grand or formal; they can be as simple as neighborhood gatherings, shared meals, or regular check-ins with friends and family. The key is that they offer a sense of belonging and connection, helping to counteract the isolation that fuels anxiety.

Rituals, too, can be powerful tools for managing anxiety. They provide structure and predictability in a chaotic and uncertain world. Whether it's a daily routine, a weekly gathering, or an annual celebration, rituals give us something to look forward to and anchor us in the present moment. They remind us that we're part of something larger than ourselves—a community, a tradition, a lineage—and that we're not alone in our struggles.

The importance of community and ritual cannot be overstated for young people, especially teenagers growing up in a digital age. They're navigating a world vastly different from the one their parents grew up in, with pressures and challenges that are often difficult for older generations to understand. Social media, while connecting them to peers across the globe, can also amplify feelings of inadequacy and anxiety. The constant comparison to others, the pressure to curate a perfect online persona, and the fear of missing out can all contribute to isolation and overwhelm.

In this context, community and ritual offer a much-needed antidote. Schools, for example, can foster a sense of community by creating spaces where students can connect meaningfully outside academics and social media pressures. These could be clubs, sports teams, or other extracurricular activities that allow students to explore their interests and build relationships in a supportive environment.

Rituals, too, can be integrated into school life, providing students with a sense of continuity and stability. Morning assemblies, graduation ceremonies, and even smaller, more personal rituals like journaling or mindfulness practices can help students feel grounded and connected. These rituals can remind them that they are part of a larger community that values and supports them.

At the societal level, we need to recognize the importance of these communal bonds and rituals and make a concerted effort to reintegrate them into our lives. This might involve rethinking how we structure our workdays, social lives, and educational systems to allow for more opportunities for connection and reflection. It might also include challenging societal norms that prioritize productivity and success at the expense of well-being and mental health.

Ultimately, the solution to our anxiety crisis lies not in isolating ourselves further or seeking out quick fixes but in reconnecting with the communal bonds and rituals that have sustained us for generations. By embracing these traditions and creating new ones that reflect our modern realities, we can build a society that supports mental health and well-being. We can create spaces where individuals feel valued, connected, and empowered to navigate life's challenges, knowing they are not alone. In doing so, we can help the anxious generation find peace and purpose in a world that often feels overwhelming and uncertain.

IMPORTANCE OF SOCIAL PRACTICES IN TEEN AND YOUNG ADULT DEVELOPMENT

In today's hyper-connected world, where screens dominate much of our daily lives, the role of media, particularly Teen TV, has taken on a new level of significance for young people. Teenagers and young adults are deeply influenced by the content they consume, especially television shows that cater specifically to their age group. These programs, often dismissed as mere entertainment, play a crucial role in shaping social behaviors and providing a blueprint for navigating the complex social landscapes of adolescence and young adulthood.

Despite this, there has been surprisingly little serious exploration of Teen TV's impact on youth development. Most discussions have focused on the importance of media literacy, urging young people to approach television critically. While this is certainly valuable, it only scratches the surface of what these shows offer regarding social learning. For teenagers, especially girls, these programs are more than just a pastime—they are a key part of how they understand and engage with the world around them.

TV dramas, comedies, and reality shows produced by networks like Nickelodeon, Disney, and MTV serve as informal guides to social life. They present scenarios that, while often dramatized for entertainment value, mirror the daily social challenges teens face. These shows offer a rehearsal space where young viewers can see different approaches to handling friendships, romantic relationships, conflicts, and the pressures of fitting in.

Consider the typical Teen TV show: characters often navigate high school dynamics, deal with peer pressure, and try to find their place in a world that feels simultaneously expansive and confining. Through these narratives, teens learn about social norms and expectations. They see the consequences of certain behaviors and the rewards of others. For instance, a character who stands up to a bully might gain respect and new friends, while one who spreads rumors might find themselves ostracized. These stories offer more than just entertainment; they provide a framework for understanding the complexities of social interactions.

This is especially important in today's digital age, where many young people's social interactions happen online, often without immediate, face-to-face feedback. Teen TV can fill in some of these gaps, showing what happens when someone posts something hurtful online and the emotional fallout that can follow. This kind of content helps young viewers develop empathy and understand the real-world implications of their actions.

Moreover, Teen TV helps adolescents develop crucial social skills. Shows often emphasize the importance of maintaining social status, understanding the unspoken rules of different social settings, and managing reputational risks. For example, a teen might learn how to navigate a tricky social situation by watching how a character on TV handles it. Whether knowing when to apologize, how to complement others without seeming insincere, or simply understanding when to stand up for oneself, these lessons are absorbed through the daily narratives that teens engage with.

In this way, Teen TV acts as a social simulator, allowing young people to explore different identities and social strategies in a low-risk environment. They can see the outcomes of various actions and learn from the characters' mistakes without having to experience the consequences themselves. This can be particularly valuable for teenagers still figuring out who they are and how they want to relate to others.

Yet, the impact of Teen TV goes beyond individual learning. These shows also contribute to the shared cultural understanding of what it means to be a teenager today. Fifteen years ago, many of us might have learned about social issues like bullying and peer pressure through Public Service Announcements (PSAs) or after-school specials. These were often didactic, straightforwardly presenting clear moral lessons. Today, those lessons are embedded in the narratives of Teen TV shows, which present more nuanced and complex portrayals of adolescence.

For instance, consider the way anxiety disorders are depicted in contemporary Teen TV. Rather than simply mocking characters who struggle with anxiety, these shows often explore the roots of their fears and the impact of mental health on their daily lives. This not only normalizes the conversation around mental health but also provides young viewers with strategies for managing their anxieties. By watching how characters on TV cope with stress—whether through therapy, talking to friends, or finding healthy outlets for their emotions—teens can pick up on valuable coping mechanisms that they might not learn elsewhere.

This shift in how we consume and engage with media reflects broader changes in our cultural understanding of adolescence. Where once we might have gathered to laugh at exaggerated portrayals of teen angst, today, we are more likely to see these characters as reflections of real challenges many young people face. The humor and drama of these shows draw us in, but the lessons they impart can have lasting effects on how teens understand themselves and their social world.

However, this is not to say that all Teen TV is inherently beneficial. As with any media, the messages can be mixed, and the portrayals of social life can sometimes reinforce harmful stereotypes or unrealistic expectations. This is where media literacy comes into play, helping teens to engage with the content they consume critically. However, rather than dismissing Teen TV outright, we should recognize its potential as a tool for social learning.

In the context of "The Anxious Generation," understanding the role of Teen TV is crucial. This generation is growing up in a world where anxiety is pervasive, fueled by both the pressures of modern life and the hyper-connected digital environment. With its mix of entertainment and social commentary, teen TV provides a way for young people to process these pressures and find their way through the challenges of adolescence. By acknowledging the value of these shows and encouraging critical engagement with them, we can help teens navigate their social worlds with greater confidence and resilience.

In the end, Teen TV's role in developing social practices among young people is a testament to the power of media in shaping how we see ourselves and others. When used wisely, it is a tool that can help guide the anxious generation through the complexities of modern life, offering them the skills and insights they need to thrive in an ever-changing world.

COMMUNITY ENGAGEMENT AND SUPPORT SYSTEMS

The power of community engagement and support systems in today's digital age cannot be overstated. Despite all the advancements in communication technology, nothing replaces the depth and warmth of genuine, face-to-face interaction. As humans, we are wired to connect on a sensory level, to feel the presence of another person, to hear the tone in their voice, and to see the concern in their eyes. These seemingly small yet profound interactions make us feel understood, supported, and valued.

In an increasingly digital world, we often lean on email, text messaging, or social media platforms to maintain our connections. While these tools offer convenience and immediacy, they sometimes need more in-person communication. For someone who feels isolated or disconnected, receiving a thoughtful message can mean the world. The knowledge that someone cares can provide immense comfort, even if the person on the receiving end cannot respond. This sense of being remembered and valued is a lifeline in a world that can often feel impersonal and isolating.

However, there comes a point when digital communication, despite its benefits, can feel limiting. The nuances of human emotion, the physical presence that conveys empathy and understanding, can sometimes get lost in the digital shuffle. When someone is struggling—whether with anxiety, depression, or the myriad of challenges life throws their way—there is something profoundly healing about knowing that another person is willing to take the time to be there in person. It's a gesture that says, "You matter enough for me to be here, to sit with you, to listen, just to be."

Physical presence can often communicate what words cannot. It's a powerful antidote to the loneliness many in our society experience. When we try to visit someone, to sit with them in their pain, we tell them, without words, that they are important, that their life has value. This kind of support is critical, especially in times of crisis. It's in these moments—when life feels unbearable—that the presence of another person can make all the difference.

This is particularly relevant when we consider the dire situations of suicide and overdose. These are not just personal tragedies but also societal failures. They highlight a desperate need for more compassion and care within our communities. Take, for instance, the situation in New Zealand, where individuals who survive an overdose may face legal penalties such as fines or imprisonment. This response is not only counterproductive but also cruel. An overdose is a cry for help, a clear indication that someone is in deep distress. Punishing them for it only adds to their suffering and pushes them further into the margins.

Instead of punishment, a system that prioritizes support and understanding is needed. When someone reaches such a point of desperation, our response as a society should be to extend a hand, not to push them down further. Community support systems must be designed to catch people before they fall too far and provide them with the resources and care they need to rebuild their lives.

Communities can play a crucial role in this. By fostering an environment of empathy and connection, communities can become the safety nets that individuals in distress desperately need. It's about creating spaces—both physical and digital—where people feel safe to express their struggles and where they know they will be met with kindness, not judgment.

Moreover, it's about recognizing that everyone has a role to play. These actions can collectively create a culture of care, whether it's checking in on a neighbor, volunteering at a local support group, or simply being present for a friend in need. This culture of care will ultimately make a difference in addressing the mental health crisis that so many young people face today.

This sense of community is particularly important for teenagers and young adults, who are often navigating complex emotions and social dynamics. The digital age offers many conveniences, but it also brings challenges—among them, the risk of feeling disconnected despite being constantly "connected." Social media can amplify feelings of inadequacy, loneliness, and anxiety, making it all the more important to counterbalance these effects with genuine human interaction.

Building strong, supportive communities can give young people the stability and sense of belonging they need to thrive. It's about teaching them that while digital connections are valuable, they should never replace the deep, meaningful relationships built in the real world. It's about showing them that they are not alone in their struggles and that a network of people is ready to support them.

Ultimately, the role of community engagement and support systems is to remind us of our shared humanity. In a world that often feels fragmented and disconnected, these systems are vital in helping us rediscover the importance of being there for one another—in person, with empathy, and without judgment. It's about creating a society where no one feels alone, everyone knows they have a place, and where we all work together to ensure that the most vulnerable are cared for and supported. This is the foundation upon which we can build a healthier, more compassionate future.

SELF-REFLECTION QUESTIONS

Do you believe you could not survive without your core relationships with peers? Why or why not?

_____

_____

_____

_____

How do these core relationships contribute to your sense of well-being and support?

_____

_____

_____

_____

Describe the community-building activity you participated in. What was its purpose, and how did you get involved?

_____

_____

_____

What activities or contributions did your peers engage in during this community-building initiative?

_____

_____

_____

After participating, do you envision yourself continuing to engage in community-building activities? Why or why not?

_____

_____

_____

_____

How has this experience influenced your perception of community involvement and its importance?

_____

_____

_____

What did you learn about yourself through this community-building activity? Did it challenge any preconceptions or reinforce specific values?

_____

_____

_____

_____

Reflect on any skills or insights gained that could be useful in future community engagements.

_____

_____

_____

_____

In your opinion, was the effort you put into participating in this community-building activity worth it? Why or why not?

_____

_____

_____

_____

How did your participation contribute to the well-being of others in the community?

_____

_____

_____

_____

Exercise:

Participate in a Community-Building Activity:

- Choose a local initiative, such as volunteering at a community garden, participating in a neighborhood cleanup, joining a local charity event, or engaging in a community awareness campaign.
- Actively participate in the chosen activity, interacting with peers and community members to contribute positively to the initiative.

Reflect on Your Experience:

- Take time to journal or discuss your experience with a trusted friend or family member.
- Consider using the self-reflection questions above to guide your thoughts and deepen your understanding of the impact of community involvement on your well-being.

Share Insights and Learn from Others:

- Explore online resources or join discussions to learn about the experiences of others who have participated in similar community-building activities.
- Share your insights and learn from diverse perspectives to enrich your understanding of community engagement and its implications.

Chapter Note

CHAPTER NINE
THE FUTURE OF CHILDHOOD AND ADOLESCENCE

"As we navigate the evolving landscape of childhood and adolescence, thoughtful consideration of technology's role is essential for shaping a balanced and healthy future." - Howard Gardner

The future of childhood and adolescence is deeply intertwined with the rapidly changing social and digital landscapes that shape young people's lives today. As society continues to evolve, so do the challenges and opportunities that define the experiences of children and teenagers. Understanding these shifts requires examining how broad social forces influence individual development, particularly in an era marked by increasing anxiety and uncertainty.

In today's world, the pressures on young people are immense. The digital age has introduced new dynamics that previous generations did not have to navigate, from the relentless presence of social media to the constant comparisons with curated online personas. These factors contribute to a growing sense of disconnection and anxiety among many young people, making it essential to rethink how we approach their development.

One of the key aspects of supporting healthy development in this context is restoring practices that foster creativity, connection, and resilience. Play, for example, has always been a fundamental part of childhood, allowing kids to explore, learn, and build social skills in a natural, unstructured environment. However, in the age of screens and digital interactions, play is increasingly being replaced by virtual experiences, which, while engaging, do not offer the same benefits as real-world play.

Encouraging play-based learning and hands-on experiences can help counteract the negative effects of excessive screen time. These activities promote critical thinking and problem-solving skills and provide a much-needed break from the pressures of performing in a digital world. By creating environments that encourage exploration and creativity, we can help children develop the emotional resilience needed to face the challenges of modern life.

Community engagement and support systems are also crucial in addressing the mental health needs of young people. As digital interactions often replace face-to-face connections, the sense of belonging and community can diminish, leading to feelings of isolation and anxiety. Building strong support networks within communities, schools, and families is essential for providing young people with the emotional and social backing they need.

These support systems can take many forms. For example, schools can implement programs that teach emotional literacy and coping skills, helping students understand and manage their feelings more effectively. Parents and educators can work together to create safe spaces for open dialogue where young people feel comfortable expressing their concerns and seeking help. These efforts are critical in creating an environment where young people feel valued and supported, helping them navigate the complexities of growing up in a digital age.

Adults, particularly parents and educators, are vital in shaping the future of childhood and adolescence. In a world where societal expectations and digital pressures can feel overwhelming, adults must be attuned to today's youth's unique challenges. This means being present, listening, and providing guidance that respects the young person's need for independence while offering the support they need to build resilience.

Adults can foster resilience by encouraging a balance between digital and real-world experiences. For instance, while expecting

188

young people to disengage from technology completely is unrealistic, enabling them to spend time in nature, engage in physical activities, and interact face-to-face can provide a healthy counterbalance to their online lives. By promoting a balanced approach, adults can help young people develop the skills they need to thrive in both digital and physical worlds.

As we consider the future of childhood and adolescence, it is clear that the challenges facing young people today are multifaceted and deeply rooted in the societal changes of our time. The pressures of modern life, including the constant pursuit of success and the high expectations placed on academic and social performance, contribute to the rising levels of anxiety among teenagers and young adults. Addressing these challenges requires a concerted effort from all of us—parents, educators, community leaders, and society.

By restoring practices that promote emotional well-being, fostering community support, and providing guidance and understanding, we can help young people develop the resilience they need to navigate the complexities of modern life. This approach addresses the immediate challenges of growing up in a digital age. It lays the foundation for a future where young people can thrive despite the world's uncertainties and pressures.

Our role in this rapidly changing world is to equip young people with the tools they need to succeed—emotional resilience, critical thinking, and a strong sense of self-worth. By focusing on these areas, we can help ensure that the next generation grows up ready to face the challenges of the digital age and capable of finding fulfillment and happiness in a world that often feels overwhelming.

Through these efforts, we can create a future where childhood and adolescence are not defined by anxiety and disconnection but by growth, learning, and the joy of discovering one's place in the world.

ADDRESSING THE DIGITAL DIVIDE AND ACCESSIBILITY

Addressing the digital divide is not just a matter of access; it's about ensuring that everyone, regardless of socioeconomic background, can fully participate in the digital world. This issue is more pressing than ever as technology becomes increasingly integral to education, employment, healthcare, and social interaction. The divide creates a barrier to inclusion, opportunity, and development, disproportionately affecting underserved communities. As global companies continue to innovate and push the latest technological advancements, the gap between those who have access and those who don't widen perpetuates inequality cycles.

The United Nations and other international bodies have long recognized the importance of bridging this divide. Former U.N. Secretary-General Kofi Annan highlighted how Information and Communication Technology (I.C.T.) can expedite development and contribute to economic growth, particularly in emerging economies. However, realizing this potential requires more than just technological innovation; it demands a concerted effort to ensure that these advancements reach everyone, especially those who have been historically marginalized.

One of the primary challenges in bridging the digital divide is the focus of major tech companies on affluent markets. These companies invest heavily in marketing to those who can afford the latest gadgets and services, while underserved communities are often overlooked. This approach not only excludes a significant portion of the global

191

population but also misses an opportunity to harness the potential of these communities in shaping the future of technology and society.

To address this, it is essential to create tailored products and services that cater to the needs of underserved populations. This means developing affordable, accessible technologies that consider these communities' unique challenges, such as limited internet access, lower levels of digital literacy, and economic constraints. It also means providing the necessary infrastructure and support to ensure these technologies can be effectively utilized.

Public Key Infrastructure (PKI) and biometrics can help enhance security and trust in digital transactions, making online resources more accessible and secure for everyone. However, implementing these technologies in underserved areas requires a thoughtful approach. It's not enough to introduce new tools; ongoing support, education, and maintenance must ensure that these communities can fully benefit from them.

Governments, tech companies, and non-governmental organizations all have a role to play in this effort. Governments can create policies and provide funding to expand digital infrastructure in underserved areas, while tech companies can invest in research and development to create affordable and accessible products. N.G.O.s can help bridge the gap by providing digital literacy training and advocating for the needs of marginalized communities.

Furthermore, addressing the digital divide requires continuous learning and adaptation. As technology evolves, so too must the strategies for ensuring equitable access. This includes staying informed about the latest technological advancements, understanding the specific needs of different communities, and being flexible enough to adjust approaches as needed.

The digital divide is not just a technological issue but a societal one. It affects how people learn, work, and interact with the world around them. By focusing on inclusion and accessibility, we can create a world where everyone has the opportunity to benefit from the digital revolution. This means ensuring that the tools and resources needed to succeed in the digital age are available to all, regardless of their background.

In practical terms, this could involve initiatives like providing free or low-cost internet access in underserved areas, offering digital literacy programs in schools and community centers, and creating platforms that are easy to use for those who are new to technology. It also means advocating for policies that promote digital inclusion at every level of government.

Ultimately, bridging the digital divide is about more than just access; it's about empowerment. It's about giving people the tools to improve their lives and contribute to their communities. It's about creating a world where technology is a force for good, driving progress and equality rather than deepening existing disparities. By taking these steps, we can build a future where everyone, regardless of their circumstances, has the chance to succeed in the digital age..

SELF-REFLECTION QUESTIONS

How do you personally feel about the concept of a technology-free community space designed for teens and young adults?

_____

_____

_____

Reflect on the potential impact of such a space on the local community. How might it benefit teens and young adults who participate?

_____

_____

_____

If you were to design this space, what specific features or activities would you include to cater to the interests and needs of teens and young adults?

_____

_____

_____

After designing and building the space, imagine observing its use by the target demographic. How closely did their activities align with your initial expectations? What surprised you the most?

_____

_____

_____

_____

If given the opportunity, what questions would you ask the teens and young adults using the space to better understand their motivations and experiences?

_____

_____

_____

Emotional Impact: Consider the emotional aspects of using a technology-free space. How might it enhance feelings of comfort, confidence, creativity, and emotional well-being among participants?

_____

_____

How important is community involvement in designing and maintaining such a space? What strategies would you employ to ensure ongoing community support?

_____

_____

Reflect on the potential long-term benefits of having a technology-free community space for teens and young adults in your local area. How might it influence their future behaviors and choices?

_____

_____

_____

Anticipate potential challenges in maintaining a technology-free environment. How would you address these challenges to ensure the space remains inviting and compelling?

_____

_____

_____

_____

Imagine yourself participating in activities within this space. How might engaging in analog activities like art projects or nature appreciation enhance your personal growth and well-being?

_____

_____

_____

Consider how this space could strengthen community bonds among different age groups (teens, young adults, older mentors). What role do intergenerational interactions play in fostering a sense of community?

_____

_____

_____

_____

Discuss the sustainability aspects of the space. How could eco-friendly practices be integrated into its design and daily operations?

_____

_____

_____

_____

Exercise:

Design and Build: Work individually or in pairs to create a detailed blueprint for the technology-free community space. Include specific activities, amenities, and environmental considerations promoting community, creativity, and well-being.

Prototype Testing:

✓ Once the space is built, invite a group of teens and young adults to use it for a specified period.

Observe their interactions and activities.

✓ Document how they utilize the space and any unexpected behaviors or activities that emerge.

Feedback and Iteration: Based on user observations and feedback, discuss potential improvements or adjustments to enhance the space's effectiveness. Consider incorporating suggestions from participants to meet their needs and preferences better.

Community Outreach: Develop a plan to engage local stakeholders (schools, community organizations, businesses) in supporting and utilizing the technology-free community space. How would you promote its benefits and encourage participation?

Diverse Programming: Brainstorm a diverse range of activities and workshops that could take place in the space. Consider creative and educational pursuits catering to various interests and skill levels.

Evaluation and Feedback: Implement a feedback mechanism to assess the space's effectiveness continuously. How would you gather user input and adjust programming based on their preferences and needs?

Promotion and Advocacy: Create a strategy to advocate for the importance of technology-free environments in promoting mental well-being and community cohesion. How would you communicate these benefits to local policymakers and community leaders?

Collaborative Design: Collaborate with local artists, educators, and community members to co-design specific elements of the space. How can their expertise contribute to creating a more engaging and welcoming environment?

Cultural Inclusivity: Explore ways to ensure the space is inclusive of diverse cultural backgrounds and perspectives. How could cultural activities and traditions be integrated into the space's programming?

Impact Assessment: Reflect on the overall impact of the space on participants' sensory experiences, personal resources, coping strategies, and emotional well-being. Discuss how the space fosters a sense of belonging, learning, growth, achievement, purpose, and happiness among users.

Chapter Note

_____

_____

_____

_____

_____

_____

_____

_____

_____

_____

_____

_____

_____

_____

_____

_____

_____

_____

_____

_____

_____

_____

_____

CHAPTER TEN
THE SAFETYISM

"An overemphasis on safety can stifle the resilience and independence that children need to thrive in an unpredictable world."

- Jonathan Haidt

This safety ethos distorts society's understanding of and response to the creation of the anxieties that are central to our human nature. An idea has taken root: child-rearing should focus on reducing generalized fearfulness. Safetyism invokes the need to shield people from the mundane challenges of life that entail risks and recognize that prolonged anxiety and overwhelmingness can diminish competence for dealing with challenges. The world – for no one's benefit – is remaking itself as such a society that elevating safety above all other spheres of life carries with it the eventual deconstruction of societal competence.

Not everything has changed. Optimism, ambition, and the fight for a better future still burn bright in our societies. Hope still abounds. But not everything has changed. One big difference is that many young people need more faith in themselves and the people and institutions around them. Many do not demonstrate the capacity to take on adult responsibilities. We (not just young people) have come to rely on third-party structures – experienced trainee counselors and community mental health services, benign closed social media networks, and protective data encryption systems – to manage our education and social care reflexes. I have called this culture of nurturing and protection "safetyism" – a disposition to elevate safety to superordinate status in behavior and garner policy support.

INTRODUCTION TO SAFETYISM

The concept of "safetyism" has gained prominence in recent years as a lens through which we can understand our growing cultural obsession with safety, risk avoidance, and anxiety management. In essence, safetyism refers to prioritizing safety above all other values, often to the detriment of other important aspects of life, such as personal growth, resilience, and freedom. This shift towards a safety-first mentality can be traced back to our evolutionary roots, where anxiety served as a critical survival mechanism. However, in today's world, where the risks are often less immediate and life-threatening, this once-useful tool has morphed into a more complex and, at times, counterproductive force.

Historically, anxiety was a natural response to environmental hazards and predator threats, key survival mechanisms for our ancestors. Imagine a prehistoric human about to explore uncharted territory—feeling anxious was not only expected but necessary. It prompted them to assess potential dangers, plan accordingly, and increase their chances of survival. This type of anxiety was functional, as it prepared individuals and their communities to face real threats, like avoiding a lion's den or navigating treacherous terrain.

While some risks remain in the modern context, the nature of threats has dramatically changed. We no longer live in a world where we must constantly guard against predators or navigate the wild without any safety nets. Instead, our anxieties have shifted towards more abstract fears—social, psychological, and existential. However, the evolutionary mechanisms that once protected us can now lead to disproportionate responses to these modern-day challenges.

For example, consider the fear of failing an exam or not getting into a prestigious college. While these are valid concerns, the intensity with which they are often experienced—by both students and parents—can be far greater than the actual consequences warrant. This hyper-anxiety can lead to overemphasizing safety and security, such as avoiding any situation where failure might be a possibility rather than embracing challenges as opportunities for growth.

In schools, this mentality can manifest in policies prioritizing emotional safety over exposure to diverse ideas and developing resilience. The rise of trigger warnings and safe spaces, while well-intentioned, can sometimes reinforce the notion that students are too fragile to cope with difficult subjects or differing opinions. This is a clear example of safetyism in action, where the desire to protect students from potential harm (emotional distress, in this case) may inadvertently limit their capacity to engage with the world fully and develop critical coping skills.

This trend extends beyond educational institutions into broader society, where an increasing focus on safety can lead to policies and cultural norms that stifle risk-taking and personal growth. For instance, the fear of litigation has led to a decline in outdoor play for children as parents and schools become increasingly cautious about potential injuries. While it's important to protect children from serious harm, overly restrictive environments can prevent them from developing the resilience and problem-solving skills that come from navigating risks independently.

Moreover, the workplace is another area where safetyism can take root. While crucial in many respects, the modern emphasis on creating 'safe' work environments can sometimes translate into an aversion to constructive criticism and honest feedback. Employees might fear speaking up or taking initiative due to potential repercussions, leading to a culture of conformity and stagnation. In such environments, the focus on avoiding psychological discomfort can undermine innovation and personal development.

To further illustrate the impact of safety, consider the rise of helicopter parenting. To protect their children from every conceivable risk, some parents micromanage their children's lives, leaving little room for independent decision-making or experiencing failure. While rooted in love and concern, this approach can hinder a child's ability to develop autonomy, resilience, and the skills necessary to navigate the complexities of adult life.

However, it is important to note that anxiety, when experienced in moderation, still serves a valuable purpose. It can motivate us to prepare for future challenges, whether studying for an important test, planning a big presentation at work, or even taking steps to secure our financial future. The key difference lies in the intensity and appropriateness of the response. Functional anxiety prompts us to take action, while hyper-anxiety can lead to avoidance, over-preparation, and a focus on controlling every possible outcome.

In the digital age, the impact of safetyism is further compounded by social media and the constant influx of information. The ability to instantly share and receive news worldwide has made us more aware of potential dangers and amplified our anxieties. Stories of rare but tragic events can dominate news cycles, leading to a skewed perception of risk and a heightened sense of vulnerability. For teenagers and young adults, who are particularly susceptible to the influences of social media, this can create a feedback loop of anxiety, where the fear of missing out or not measuring up to their peers exacerbates their stress levels.

The challenge, then, is to find a balance that acknowledges the importance of safety without allowing it to overshadow other critical aspects of life. As we navigate this increasingly complex world, it's essential to recognize that some degree of risk is unavoidable and necessary for growth. Encouraging resilience, promoting open dialogue, and fostering environments where it's safe to take risks and make mistakes are all crucial steps in countering the negative effects of safety.

In conclusion, while safety and anxiety are rooted in evolutionary survival mechanisms, applying these instincts in today's world can sometimes do more harm than good. By understanding the role of safetyism in shaping our behaviors and societal norms, we can begin to challenge the excessive emphasis on risk avoidance and work towards creating a more balanced approach that promotes personal growth, resilience, and genuine well-being.

IMPACT ON CHILDHOOD DEVELOPMENT

The concept of "safetyism" has become increasingly relevant in recent years, particularly when considering the mental health challenges faced by the younger generation in the digital age. This term encapsulates the cultural shift toward prioritizing safety, risk avoidance, and anxiety management, above all other values, sometimes at the expense of personal growth, resilience, and freedom. While safety has roots in our evolutionary history—where anxiety played a crucial role in survival—it has morphed into a more complex and often counterproductive force in today's society, especially for teenagers and young adults.

Historically, anxiety was a functional response to environmental hazards and predator threats, ensuring our ancestors were cautious and prepared for danger. Imagine a prehistoric human about to explore uncharted territory; anxiety would prompt them to assess potential risks and increase their chances of survival. This type of anxiety was not just useful; it was necessary for the survival of the individual and their community.

However, the nature of threats has dramatically changed in the modern context. We no longer face the same immediate physical dangers, but our anxieties have shifted towards more abstract social, psychological, and existential fears. These new forms of anxiety, while still rooted in our evolutionary mechanisms, often lead to disproportionate responses to modern-day challenges. Teenagers and young adults navigating a world shaped by rapid technological advancements and constant social media connectivity can result in an overwhelming sense of vulnerability and fear.

Take, for example, the anxiety surrounding academic performance. The fear of failing an exam or not getting into a prestigious college can be intense for students and their parents. While these concerns are valid, the level of anxiety often exceeds the actual consequences. This hyper-anxiety can lead to overemphasizing safety and security, where students might avoid any situation where failure is possible rather than embracing challenges as opportunities for growth. This mindset can be detrimental, limiting their ability to develop the resilience needed to cope with life's inevitable setbacks.

In educational settings, safety can manifest in policies prioritizing emotional safety over exposure to diverse ideas and experiences. The rise of trigger warnings and safe spaces, while intended to protect students from potential harm, can sometimes reinforce the notion that they are too fragile to cope with difficult subjects or differing opinions. This protective approach, although well-meaning, may inadvertently stifle the development of critical coping skills and limit students' capacity to engage fully with the world around them.

Beyond schools, the culture of safetyism extends into broader society, influencing policies and cultural norms that discourage risk-taking and personal growth. For instance, the fear of litigation has led to a decline in outdoor play for children as parents and schools become increasingly cautious about potential injuries. While protecting children from serious harm is important, overly restrictive environments can prevent them from developing the problem-solving skills and resilience that come from navigating risks independently.

In the workplace, safetyism can manifest as an aversion to constructive criticism and honest feedback. The modern emphasis on creating "safe" work environments—while crucial in many respects— can sometimes lead to a culture of conformity and stagnation, where employees fear speaking up or taking the initiative due to potential repercussions. In such environments, the focus on avoiding psychological discomfort can undermine innovation and personal development.

The impact of safetyism is also evident in parenting styles, particularly with the rise of helicopter parenting. To protect their children from every conceivable risk, some parents micromanage their children's lives, leaving little room for independent decision-making or the experience of failure. While this approach is rooted in love and concern, it can hinder a child's ability to develop autonomy, resilience, and the skills necessary to navigate the complexities of adult life.

In the digital age, safetyism is further compounded by the influence of social media. The ability to instantly share and receive news from around the world has made us more aware of potential dangers, but it has also amplified our anxieties. Stories of rare but tragic events can dominate news cycles, leading to a skewed perception of risk and a heightened sense of vulnerability. For teenagers and young adults, who are particularly susceptible to the influences of social media, this can create a feedback loop of anxiety, where the fear of missing out or not measuring up to their peers exacerbates their stress levels.

The challenge, then, is to find a balance that acknowledges the importance of safety without allowing it to overshadow other critical aspects of life. As we navigate this increasingly complex world, it's essential to recognize that some degree of risk is unavoidable and necessary for growth. Encouraging resilience, promoting open dialogue, and fostering environments where it's safe to take risks and make mistakes are all crucial steps in countering the negative effects of safety.

While anxiety, in moderation, still serves a valuable purpose—motivating us to prepare for future challenges and take proactive steps to secure our well-being—hyper-anxiety can lead to avoidance, over-preparation, and an unhealthy focus on controlling every possible outcome. This is particularly relevant in the context of the digital age, where the constant influx of information and the pressures of social media can exacerbate feelings of inadequacy and fear among young people.

In conclusion, while safety and anxiety are rooted in evolutionary survival mechanisms, applying these instincts in today's world can sometimes do more harm than good. By understanding the role of safetyism in shaping our behaviors and societal norms, particularly in the lives of teenagers and young adults, we can begin to challenge the excessive emphasis on risk avoidance and work towards creating a more balanced approach that promotes personal growth, resilience, and genuine well-being.

CASE STUDIES AND EXAMPLES

The effort to mitigate fear of violent crime by embedding police officers in schools is a complex issue with far-reaching consequences. It's a response that has gained substantial support from government bodies and concerned parents, aiming to bolster school security. However, this well-intentioned approach often overlooks the deeper socio-economic factors that contribute to the criminalization of children, leading to unintended negative outcomes.

Let's consider Timothy, a school officer stationed at a large urban public school. Timothy's daily responsibilities include monitoring student behavior, enforcing policies, and ensuring a safe school environment. On the surface, this may seem like a practical solution to a very real problem. However, Timothy's role extends beyond mere security; it bleeds into policing student behavior in ways that educators and school administrators traditionally handled.

Timothy's presence at the school is part of a broader trend known as the "school-to-prison pipeline," where disciplinary policies and practices push students, particularly those from marginalized communities, out of schools and into the criminal justice system. The introduction of police officers into schools initially intended to prevent violence, often leads to the excessive criminalization of minor infractions. Students are subjected to the authority of police officers for actions that, in previous generations, would have been handled internally by school staff.

One of the most alarming aspects of this shift is how it reshapes school culture. The proliferation of armed security, metal detectors, and zero-tolerance policies for weapons contribute to an environment that feels more like a correctional facility than a place of learning. While these measures are designed to enhance safety, they also create a climate of fear and suspicion, where students are constantly monitored and their behavior is scrutinized.

This culture of heightened security, often referred to as "fortress-style schools," has significant implications for these institutions' educational mission. The focus on safety at all costs can overshadow the primary goal of education, which is to foster intellectual growth, critical thinking, and social development. Instead of creating a nurturing environment where students feel valued and supported, these policies can make them feel like suspects in their schools.

Timothy's case also highlights a broader societal issue: the decline of civic obligation and the erosion of trust between young people and state institutions. By placing police officers in schools and relying on them to manage student behavior, we are effectively outsourcing the role of educators in guiding and governing students. This shift undermines the authority of teachers and administrators and diminishes the role of education as a means of socialization and civic engagement.

Moreover, the reliance on police officers in schools often disproportionately affects students of color and those from low-income backgrounds. These students are more likely to be disciplined, suspended, or arrested for behavior that might be overlooked or handled differently in more affluent schools. This disparity exacerbates existing inequalities and reinforces a cycle of disadvantage, where marginalized students are more likely to be funneled into the criminal justice system.

To better understand the impact of these policies, we can also examine the experience of a large urban school district that implemented zero-tolerance policies in response to a highly publicized incident of school violence. The district installed metal detectors hired additional security personnel and introduced strict disciplinary measures to maintain order. While these changes were initially praised for making schools safer, they also had unintended consequences.

Students reported feeling alienated and distrusted by the institutions that were supposed to support them. The emphasis on punitive measures rather than restorative practices led to a sharp increase in suspensions and expulsions, particularly among minority students. The school environment became more tense and adversarial, with students and staff feeling the pressure of constant surveillance.

This case study underscores the need for a more nuanced approach to school safety, which recognizes the importance of creating a supportive and inclusive environment for all students. Rather than relying on police officers and punitive measures, schools should invest in resources that address the root causes of violence and misbehavior. This could include hiring more counselors and social workers, implementing restorative justice programs, and training teachers and administrators on managing conflict and supporting students' emotional needs.

Additionally, engaging students, parents, and communities in conversations about school safety is crucial. By involving these stakeholders in the decision-making process, schools can develop policies that reflect the needs and concerns of those most affected by these changes. This collaborative approach can help build trust and foster a sense of shared responsibility for students' well-being.

In conclusion, while the presence of police officers in schools may offer a sense of security, it is essential to examine this approach's broader implications critically. The criminalization of student behavior, the decline of civic engagement, and the reinforcement of social inequalities are significant concerns that must be addressed. By rethinking our approach to school safety and creating supportive and inclusive environments, we can better serve the needs of all students and help them thrive academically and personally.

PROPOSED SOLUTIONS

Redefine the Fear of Modern Society:

Modern society has become increasingly gripped by a pervasive fear of crime, leading to heightened levels of blame, hyper-vigilance, and a loss of trust in our communities. This fear distracts us from the potential joys of collective life and diminishes our ability to see the good that can be achieved when people come together. The societal obsession with safety and security has eroded childhood freedoms and replaced them with a cynical view of the world, which projects weariness and mistrust into public life.

Research shows that social connectedness is key to achieving positive health outcomes. Recognizing this, governments have an opportunity to create policies that strengthen community bonds and foster resilience. By investing in a wide range of activities and educational programs tailored to the unique needs of local communities, governments can empower individuals to form meaningful connections. These connections are crucial in promoting a sense of belonging and well-being, which serves as a buffer against isolation and the associated mental health issues.

Schools play an essential role in this effort by promoting strong social bonds among students. Schools must take active steps to integrate cooperative values into their curriculum, emphasizing the importance of relationships and teaching that individual success is tied to the success of others. The educational approach should focus on more than just academic achievements; it should also foster socioemotional learning. By nurturing these skills, schools can help students navigate human interactions with empathy and respect, thereby preparing them to build a society based on trust, mutual respect, and a shared sense of purpose.

Redefining our collective perception of fear requires a shift in mindset. By acknowledging the power of social connectedness and striving to strengthen it, governments and schools can lead the way toward a more trusting, respectful, and united society. Embracing the rewards of community life allows us to move beyond fear and toward a brighter, more inclusive future.

Shift the Curriculum and Routine:

Transforming the curriculum and routine in educational settings can profoundly impact children's development and overall well-being. Numerous studies have shown that incorporating alternative curricula and routines can significantly enhance children's cognitive, emotional, and social growth. To truly nurture the whole child, educational curricula should expand beyond traditional subjects to include various topics and activities.

Modern curricula should take a holistic approach, including subjects like nature education to foster environmental stewardship, drama to encourage self-expression, physical activity to promote health, and music and art to spark creativity. In addition to academic subjects, core values such as kindness, compassion, gratitude, and respect should be woven into every aspect of classroom activities. These values shape character and teach children the importance of working together and supporting one another.

Schools' daily routines should also be reimagined to allow for more free play, creative exploration, and unstructured time. Open-ended activities and play are essential for cultivating curiosity, problem-solving skills, and independent thinking. By providing time for these activities, schools can help children develop the confidence and resilience they need to face challenges in the future.

Moreover, it is crucial to prioritize social and emotional learning within the school routine. Children need guidance in managing emotions, building healthy relationships, and communicating effectively. Life skill training, such as critical thinking, problem-solving, decision-making, time management, and communication, should also be integrated into the daily schedule. These skills are vital for preparing children to navigate the complexities of the modern world.

By shifting the curriculum and routine, we can create educational environments that support children's holistic development. By embracing diverse subjects, fostering core values, and allowing time for unstructured play and life skill development, schools can help children flourish academically, emotionally, and socially. These changes will enable the next generation to grow into well-rounded individuals equipped to thrive in an ever-changing world.

SELF-REFLECTION QUESTION

Reflect on your own childhood experiences with safety regulations. How did safety concerns manifest in your daily life at home and school?

_____

_____

_____

_____

_____

Consider current safety measures in schools, playgrounds, and community spaces. How do you perceive these regulations? Do you believe they adequately protect children, or do they sometimes hinder their development?

_____

_____

_____

_____

_____

How have safety regulations impacted your views on children's independence, risk-taking behaviors, and resilience? Have you observed instances where safety concerns limited opportunities for exploration and growth?

_____

_____

_____

_____

_____

_____

Exercise:

Reflect on personal experiences with safety regulations and propose strategies for promoting a balanced approach to child safety. Based on your reflections from the self-reflection questions:

Write down your thoughts on how safety regulations affected your childhood and how they impact children today.

_____

_____

_____

_____

_____

_____

Brainstorm and list potential strategies or changes that could be made to safety policies to better balance protection with fostering independence and growth in children.

_____

_____

_____

_____

_____

_____

_____

_____

Develop an action plan outlining steps you can take personally or within your community to advocate for a more balanced approach to child safety.

_____

_____

_____

_____

_____

_____

CHAPTER ELEVEN
THE DECLINE OF PLAY

"The decline of play in children's lives not only hinders their development but also deprives them of essential skills for creativity and social interaction."

- Peter Gray

The decline of play in modern childhood is a troubling trend that reflects deeper issues in our society's approach to early development. In the United States, children now spend an alarming six to eight hours per day in front of screens, not counting the time they spend on homework. This shift has significant implications for young minds' cognitive, emotional, and physical development. Rather than encouraging free play—a crucial component of healthy childhood development—many preschools now focus on structured, purposeful activities to optimize academic outcomes. As a result, most forms of play have been eliminated from these educational environments, leaving little room for creativity and imagination to flourish.

This trend isn't limited to the U.S.; it is rapidly spreading across Europe and has taken hold in the United Kingdom, signaling a broader societal shift prioritizing academic achievement over children's holistic development. The irony is that while we push children towards structured learning, we inadvertently stifle the qualities—creativity, problem-solving, and emotional resilience—essential for success in life. The modern generation of preschoolers, with their minimal outdoor time and restricted opportunities for unstructured play, is on track to become the least active cohort in human history.

The consequences of this shift are profound. Play is not just a frivolous activity; it is a fundamental way through which children explore the world, develop social skills, and build the foundations of their future selves. The absence of play limits children's ability to experiment, take risks, and learn from failure in a safe environment.

These experiences are critical for developing the resilience needed to navigate the complexities of life.

The decline of play also mirrors the growing anxiety and stress that children and their parents experience in today's world. As society becomes more competitive and results-driven, the pressure to succeed starts earlier and earlier. Parents, driven by a fear of their children falling behind, often push them into structured activities that leave little room for free play. This cycle of anxiety and control not only affects children's development but also contributes to the increasing rates of anxiety and depression among young people.

A poignant example of the power of unstructured play comes from a story in 1981 when a series of preschools were built in a poverty-stricken neighborhood of Chicago. These preschools were designed to counter the influence of television and provide children with a stimulating environment filled with various activities. Yet, when the children were given a tour of these vibrant, activity-filled rooms, they were most drawn to a single, empty room. Despite the adults' expectations that the other rooms, filled with toys and learning materials, would captivate the children, the empty room held their attention.

In this unadorned space, the children found something that structured activities could not offer: freedom. Without the distractions of toys and materials designed to guide their play, they were free to use their imaginations, invent games, and explore the possibilities that unstructured space offered. This empty room became a sanctuary of creativity and self-directed exploration, highlighting the deep, innate need for play that structured environments often overlook.

This story powerfully reminds us of what we lose when we eliminate play from children's lives. In our quest to prepare children for the future, we risk depriving them of the experiences that prepare them for the uncertainties of life. Play is not just about fun; it is about developing children's skills and resilience to face challenges, solve problems, and connect with others.

As we move further into the digital age, it is essential to remember the importance of play in childhood development. Screens and structured activities cannot replace the rich, sensory experiences of interacting with the physical world. To nurture a generation of well-rounded, emotionally healthy individuals, we must prioritize play and ensure children have the time and space to explore, imagine, and create on their own terms.

The story of the empty room is a metaphor for what children truly need—a space where they can be free from the pressures of performance and expectation, a space where they can be children. It is a call to action for parents, educators, and society to reclaim the importance of play in our children's lives and recognize that in doing so, we are giving them the tools they need to thrive in an increasingly complex and demanding world.

In my circled world, the 70- and 80-somethings reared in nurturing suburban and small-town community environments cut me slack that I cannot reciprocate. As a seasoned psychotherapist with four decades of experience, I have been entrusted by countless clients who have shared their most profound and most excruciating life stories, entrusting me with their vulnerabilities as they present themselves as competent and compassionate adults. For the longest time, I found myself swift to pass judgment upon those who fulfill roles as parents, coaches, referees, and teachers to young children, accusing them of excessive hovering and suffocating their kids with an abundance of protective measures, effectively suffocating the very essence of life from them.

There were several concrete reasons for my harshness and unwavering stance on steering children away from the demands of structured year-round sports and activities. This conviction was not arbitrary; it was rooted in my thorough examination of the extensive research that consistently showed how an excess of a supposedly positive thing could become detrimental. Living in an era characterized by relentless pressure, where parents were constantly grappling with the financial burdens of the gradual disappearance of safety nets, I understood the need for caution. The omnipresent and fear-inducing media flooded our living rooms with the most distressing and horrifying news, intensifying the already existing anxiety. As a result, countless professionals in their twenties and thirties found themselves desperately trying to juggle numerous responsibilities, attempting to achieve the impossible feat of having it all while maintaining an unprecedented pace of life. For these individuals, being able to dedicate precious moments to their children, particularly on a tranquil Saturday morning at a soccer field, served as a form of respite. It was an opportunity to exhale and escape the fierce demands of daily existence momentarily. However, tragically, this fleeting respite often came at a steep cost. The elusive concept of "me" time, crucial for maintaining balance and personal well-being, was frequently sacrificed without mercy.

Consequently, my insistence on prioritizing children's well-being and psychological welfare over the pressures of excessive extracurricular activities was born out of genuine concern. I firmly believed that it was imperative to find a delicate equilibrium to protect the sanctity of both childhood and the parent-child relationship. It was essential to balance providing enriching opportunities for growth and ensuring that the overwhelming pace of life consumed only some available moments, leaving no room for self-reflection and rejuvenation.

TECHNOLOGICAL AND SOCIAL INFLUENCES

In today's fast-paced, technology-driven world, there's a growing concern about the mental health of children and adolescents, particularly the rise in anxiety and depression. This anxiety epidemic is often overlooked, as its causes are deeply embedded in the structures and expectations of modern life. At the heart of this issue lies a troubling shift in how childhood is experienced and understood—away from the freedom and spontaneity of play and towards an environment dominated by structured activities, academic pressures, and a constant push for perfection.

One of the most damaging influences on young people's mental health today is the way our society has redefined what it means to be a successful child. From an early age, children are bombarded with messages that equate their worth with their academic achievements, particularly their ability to excel in standardized tests. The pursuit of perfect scores and the constant pressure to perform at an exceptionally high level creates a fertile ground for anxiety and depression. This relentless focus on academic success leaves little room for the unstructured, self-directed play crucial for healthy cognitive and emotional development.

Free play—play initiated and led by children without adult intervention—is vital for developing creativity, problem-solving skills, and emotional resilience. However, free play is increasingly under threat in the current cultural landscape. The lives of children today are often tightly scheduled, with little opportunity for them to engage in the kind of imaginative, open-ended activities that were once a staple of childhood. This shift is driven by various factors, including the belief that early academic success is the key to future prosperity and a broader societal trend towards over-structuring children's lives to protect them from perceived dangers and ensure they are well-prepared for a competitive world.

This cultural shift is not just affecting children; it's also reshaping the lives of adults, particularly parents. Many of today's parents grew up when childhood was less structured, with more opportunities for unstructured play and exploration. However, the pressures of modern life, including the demands of work, the pace of technological change, and the societal expectations placed on parents, have led to a lifestyle that leaves little room for the kind of free time that fosters creativity and resilience. As a result, both children and adults find themselves trapped in a cycle of constant busyness, with few opportunities to disconnect and recharge.

The consequences of this shift are profound. With time for free play, children can develop important life skills, such as the ability to entertain themselves, solve problems independently, and manage their emotions. This lack of play contributes to the rise in anxiety and depression, as children are left feeling overwhelmed by the pressures of a world that demands constant achievement. Moreover, the lack of downtime in adult life means that parents are often too stressed and overcommitted to provide the supportive, relaxed environment children need to thrive.

In the digital age, these pressures are amplified by the constant presence of social media and technology. Modern life is always connected, so children and adults are constantly bombarded with information, much of it reinforcing the idea that success is measured by external achievements rather than personal fulfillment. This environment fosters a culture of comparison, where children and parents alike are pressured to keep up with the perceived successes of others, further fueling feelings of inadequacy and anxiety.

This shift in how we structure our lives and raise our children is deeply intertwined with the themes explored in this book. The relentless pursuit of academic success and the over-scheduling of children's lives are symptomatic of a broader societal trend towards safetyism. In this cultural phenomenon, avoiding risk and pursuing security are prioritized above all else. In this context, the traditional, unstructured play vital for healthy development is seen as a luxury rather than a necessity.

The implications of this trend are far-reaching. By focusing so heavily on academic achievement and structured activities, we inadvertently deprive children of the experiences they need to develop into well-rounded, resilient individuals. At the same time, we are also placing undue stress on parents, who are expected to manage their children's lives in a way that leaves little room for spontaneity or relaxation. This cycle of anxiety and over-commitment is unsustainable, and it is contributing to the rising rates of mental health issues among both children and adults.

We must re-evaluate our approach to childhood and parenting to address these challenges. This means recognizing the value of free play and unstructured time for children and adults. It also means pushing back against the cultural pressures that equate success with academic achievement and constant busyness. By creating more opportunities for play, relaxation, and genuine connection, we can help reduce the levels of anxiety and depression that are so prevalent in today's society.

In conclusion, the decline of free play and the rise of structured, achievement-oriented childhoods are key factors driving the anxiety epidemic among young people today. To counter these trends, we must re-emphasize the importance of play and unstructured time in children's and adults' lives. Only by doing so can we begin to address the root causes of the mental health crisis and create a healthier, more balanced society.

HEALTH AND DEVELOPMENTAL BENEFITS

Play-based learning is more than just a fun activity for children—it's a powerful tool that sets the foundation for lifelong happiness, independence, and success. When children engage in play, they tap into their innate curiosity and creativity, which is essential for developing rich imaginations and forming meaningful relationships. These moments of the game and exploration are not just about passing the time; they are about building the skills and attitudes that will carry them through life.

Psychologist Mihály Csíkszentmihályi coined the term "flow" to describe the mental state where a person is fully immersed in an activity, experiencing intense concentration and a sense of enjoyment. This concept is especially relevant when considering how children learn and develop. When children are given the freedom to play, they often enter this state of flow, deeply engaging in activities that captivate their attention and bring them joy. This state is pleasurable and highly productive, as it allows children to learn new skills, solve problems creatively, and build confidence in their abilities.

Incorporating play-based methods into education is not just about making learning more enjoyable—it's about unlocking each child's full potential. These methods encourage children to take risks, explore new ideas, and develop a love for learning that will stay with them throughout their lives. When children are allowed to follow their passions and engage in activities that interest them, they are more likely to experience flow, which Csíkszentmihályi argues is the key to personal fulfillment and creativity. This approach to learning is about more than just academic success; it's about helping children become well-rounded individuals capable of thinking critically, solving problems, and navigating the complexities of life with confidence and resilience.

Parents who recognize the value of play understand that it is a powerful tool for reducing stress and creating a positive home environment. Play creates a safe space where children can be themselves, make mistakes, and learn without fear of judgment. This environment of acceptance and encouragement is crucial for their emotional development, as it helps them build resilience and develop the skills they need to face challenges in the future.

When families incorporate play, laughter, and storytelling into their daily routines, they create a nurturing environment that strengthens family bonds and enhances communication. These shared experiences are enjoyable and vital for emotional healing and growth. By making time for play, families can transform daily life into something more harmonious and connected, reducing stress and promoting a sense of well-being that benefits everyone in the household.

In today's fast-paced, pressure-filled world, children are often expected to conform to rigid standards and excel in various areas. The demands placed on them can be overwhelming, and the pressure to succeed can stifle their natural creativity and curiosity. However, when children are encouraged to approach learning with playfulness and exploration, they develop the flexibility and creativity needed to navigate these demands successfully.

Challenges do not deter a child who is passionate about learning; instead, they see them as opportunities to grow and learn. These children are more likely to take initiative, manage their time effectively, and reflect on their progress, all of which are essential skills for success in school and beyond. When students can explore their interests and pursue their passions, they are more engaged in their education and more likely to develop the skills and attitudes to help them succeed.

The benefits of play extend beyond childhood and into adulthood. Adults who grew up in environments that valued play and creativity are often better equipped to handle the stresses and challenges of modern life. They are more likely to be resilient, adaptable, and capable of thinking outside the box. In a constantly changing world, these skills are more important than ever.

As we think about the future of education and child development, it's clear that play should be at the center of our approach. By valuing and encouraging play, we can help children develop into happy, independent, and successful adults committed to lifelong learning. Play-based methods are not just a way to make learning more enjoyable—they are vital to helping children reach their full potential and lead fulfilling lives.

CULTURAL SHIFTS IN PARENTING

There has been a noticeable shift in parental attitudes towards play in recent years, reflecting broader cultural changes that impact children's development and well-being. This transformation in parenting styles, characterized by trends such as "helicopter parenting" and "snowplow parents," has altered the traditional role of play in childhood, often reducing opportunities for unsupervised and spontaneous activities. This change stems from a collective concern among parents who worry about their children's safety and success, leading them to micromanage their children's lives in ways that may hinder the development of independence and resilience.

"Helicopter parenting" is a style in which parents closely monitor and intervene in their children's activities to ensure their safety and success. While this approach comes from a place of love and concern, it can have unintended consequences. Children raised under such intense supervision may struggle to develop the essential skills for self-reliance and problem-solving. The fear of letting children experience the world independently has led to a decline in free play, crucial for fostering creativity, social skills, and emotional regulation.

The phenomenon of "snowplow parenting" takes this a step further, with parents actively removing obstacles from their children's paths to ensure a smooth journey. This practice, while well-intentioned, can lead to the ill-prepared need to prepare for the inevitable challenges of adulthood. Without the opportunity to encounter and overcome difficulties, children may develop a heightened sense of anxiety and a reduced capacity to cope with stress. This approach can also contribute to childhood burnout, where children are overwhelmed by the pressure to succeed in multiple areas, from academics to extracurricular activities.

An interesting aspect to consider is the potential link between the rise in childhood anxiety and the over-scheduling of children's lives. The relentless pursuit of academic and extracurricular success, often driven by parents' fears of falling behind, can make children feel overwhelmed and anxious. This anxiety can manifest in various ways, including physical symptoms like colic in infants or burnout in older children. The pressure to excel in every aspect of life leaves little room for the unstructured, imaginative play vital for healthy development.

In exploring alternative approaches to parenting, the concept of "loose parts play" has emerged as a promising counterbalance to these modern parenting trends. Loose parts play involves providing children with various materials—such as stones, sticks, or recycled objects—that they can use creatively without specific instructions or outcomes. This type of play encourages children to use their imagination, develop problem-solving skills, and engage in cooperative play with others. It allows for a return to a more natural form of play that is child-led and free from the constraints of adult expectations.

The rise of loose parts play reflects a growing recognition among some parents that children need opportunities for unstructured play to develop into well-rounded individuals. This approach fosters a sense of community and connection among families who embrace it, as they are committed to allowing their children the freedom to explore and learn at their own pace. By prioritizing play that is flexible and responsive to the moment, parents and children alike can experience the joy and creativity that comes from engaging with the world on their own terms.

The influence of technology on parenting is another significant factor in the decline of free play. As technology becomes more integrated into daily life, parents and children spend more time in front of screens and less time engaging in physical and outdoor activities. This shift has contributed to a culture where structured, screen-based activities often replace the free play that previous generations took for granted. The constant connectivity offered by technology also exacerbates the fear of missing out (FOMO), making parents feel compelled to fill their children's schedules with organized activities rather than allowing them the freedom to play spontaneously.

One notable example of how these cultural shifts have impacted parenting is the response to the social disturbances in the United Kingdom in August 2011. In the aftermath of these events, the government faced criticism for its decision to cut funding for youth centers as part of austerity measures. These centers provided vital spaces for young people to engage in positive activities and build social connections. The decision to close them highlighted how societal priorities, driven by economic concerns, can undermine the support systems crucial for children's development.

The work of influential psychoanalysts like Winnicott has also shed light on the changing landscape of childhood. Winnicott argued that childhood's essential aspects are lost in modern society, where the focus has shifted from nurturing a child's natural development to managing their every move. He emphasized the importance of allowing children the space to grow and explore independently, free from the constant oversight of adults.

In conclusion, the cultural shifts in parenting reflect broader societal changes that have reshaped the role of play in childhood. The rise of helicopter and snowplow parenting, driven by fear and anxiety, has led to a decline in free play and an increase in structured, adult-led activities. However, the emergence of movements like loose parts play offers a hopeful counterbalance, encouraging a return to child-led, imaginative play that fosters independence and creativity. As parents and society continue to navigate these changes, it is essential to recognize the value of play in supporting children's overall well-being and development.

SELF-REFLECTION QUESTIONS

What play activities did you engage in as a child that you found most enjoyable and beneficial? How did these activities help you develop creativity, social skills, and problem-solving abilities?

_____

_____

_____

_____

_____

_____

_____

Think about children you know or have observed. What types of play do they engage in? How do these activities compare to the play experiences you had?

_____

_____

_____

_____

_____

_____

_____

How do digital devices and screen time affect children's playtime today? Does technology enhance or hinder their creativity, social interaction, and problem-solving skills?

_____

_____

_____

_____

What are some common barriers that prevent children from engaging in play-based activities (e.g., lack of time, space, safety concerns, or societal pressures)? How can these barriers be addressed?

_____

_____

_____

_____

_____

Why do you believe play is essential for children's development? How do you see play contributing to their overall growth and well-being?

_____

_____

_____

_____

_____

Exercise:

Brainstorm and Plan Play-Based Activities

Activity Brainstorming:

List at least five play-based activities that would foster children's creativity, social interaction, and problem-solving skills. Consider various activities, including outdoor games, arts and crafts, role-playing scenarios, and team-building exercises.

1._____

2._____

3._____

4._____

5._____

Detailed Activity Planning:

Select two activities from your list and create a detailed plan for each. Include the following elements:

✓ **Activity Name:** Give the activity a fun and engaging name.

✓ **Objectives**: Outline the main goals of the activity (e.g., promoting teamwork, encouraging imaginative thinking).

✓ **Materials Needed:** List any materials or equipment required.

✓ **Step-by-Step Instructions:** Provide clear instructions on how to set up and conduct the activity.

✓ **Age Group:** Specify the appropriate age group for the activity.

✓ Safety Considerations: Identify any safety precautions or considerations to keep in mind.

CONCLUSION

As cognitive (or other) therapies are shown to relieve sufferers of panic disorder, agoraphobia, school, and generalized anxiety, as well as other anxiety disorders such as social phobia (as described previously), the doors of society can open more for these worried people to step through. The Human Rights Act 1998 enshrines everyone's inalienable right to a peaceful life, and anxiety - in whatever form - delivers a life sentence of (at best) worry. To learn to be calm, to live life naturally, to help society correctly diagnose - or adjudicate (through a clinical professional) against suicide, need the least amount of therapy and the most significant amount of help (from valid, reliable, and validly reliable sources).

At the same time as being cautious - in making sure we do not pathologize (excessive) normal behavior or in applying the disease to self and others when a "normal" identity crisis could exist - the clinical professions and society, in general, should also be vigilant of a trend for underdiagnosing and under-treating anxiety disorder. Two of our high-risk groups are children and older people, but they are also the hardest to get into treatment in any routine sense. They are also the groups that best exemplify why change is needed. Where children are concerned, the figures are telling. Over 5% of children are suffering from anxiety and its effects, but nearly 90% of children with a clinical anxiety disorder never receive treatment. It appears that only 15% of sufferers of anxiety-related problems get help. Sufferers from agoraphobia, insomnia, and panic or anxiety disorder show a similar profile of less than one in six seeking treatment. At the other end of the spectrum, older people lack access to clinical services.

SUMMARIZING KEY FINDINGS AND INSIGHTS

Anxiety disorders are common and, by their very nature, are associated with much morbidity. However, they are also treatable but are often ineffectively treated or not recognized and treated at all. The providers of medical care frequently trivialize the conditions and are usually dismissive of their celebrity, "over-diagnosing it and medicalizing the human condition." Worse still, they may only address part of the problem, such as the depressive aspects of the condition, and therefore cause considerable morbidity. For the condition of Generalised Anxiety Disorder (G.A.D.), a heavily medicalized condition can be appropriate. What may appear by some to be over-treatment (plasma concentrations far exceeding those now recommended), and there are numerous accounts of patients who take medications who remain self-assessed as being over-anxious, can frequently be inadequate treatment. Cognitive behavioral therapies are undoubtedly superior as direct treatment for many of the group of disorders covered by the DSM-IV diagnosis of anxiety.

Anxiety disorders are the most typical and most treatable mental health conditions. However, they remain under-diagnosed and under-treated, perhaps due to misunderstanding as to what these conditions represent. This misunderstanding probably contributes to some of the stigma attached, with expressions about individuals simply needing to pull themselves together being entirely unhelpful. This two-part lecture seeks to put right some of the misconceptions by describing the range and variety of anxious states, the environmental and biological contributors to the development of these states, and the systems that need to go awry to produce different sorts of anxiety. These biological systems, and Damien Hirst's The Biology of Fear combined with other animal models, afford insight into how best to provide innovative, better tolerated, new treatments. They may also help develop potential screening tools to make early intervention possible.

Call to Action for a Healthier Future for Teens and Young Adults

The increase in rates of anxiety among teens and young adults in our American society is a sign that something is going awry. The use of anti-anxiety drugs and long waiting times for access to mental health social workers in colleges indicate that these issues are potentially evolving into a public health crisis. The college students of today are our workers and parents of the future. Parents must teach their children essential life skills and negotiate with them to prevent too much and too frequent use of electronic devices. Parents must keep open channels of communication and speak openly and honestly about negative qualities and qualities that can improve mental health. Social groups may produce genetic diversity, but will an increase in the number of heal or exacerbate the problems? Many programs in higher education campuses bring students together based on genetics, sexuality, etc., thus encouraging students to divide themselves based on these qualities. As schools increasingly emphasize the need for students to form groups and learn interpersonal skills, are adequate resources or research providing what is required to accomplish the goal?

Chapter Note

THANK YOU

Dear Reader,

Writing "Anxious Generation" has been an enriching journey that would not have been possible without the support and encouragement of many outstanding individuals.

First and foremost, I extend my deepest gratitude to my family. Your unwavering belief in me has been my most significant source of strength and motivation. Thank you for your patience, understanding, and love throughout this process.

To my readers, past and present, thank you for inspiring me every day. Your insights and experiences have shaped the ideas in this book and have been instrumental in its creation.

I am profoundly grateful to my colleagues and mentors, who have generously shared their wisdom and offered invaluable feedback. Your guidance has been pivotal in shaping this work.

Thanks to the editorial team, whose dedication and attention to detail have helped refine this manuscript. Your commitment to excellence is deeply appreciated.

Thank you all for being a part of this remarkable journey. Your support and encouragement have made "Anxious Generation" possible.

With heartfelt gratitude,

Frankie A. Albury

alburyfrankie@gmail.com/dennisdaviskf@gmail.com

Kindly scan the above **QR** code
and enjoy
Work-Balance Workbook

Kindly scan the above QR code
and enjoy
Coping Strategies for Anxiety

Kindly scan the above **QR code**
and enjoy
Sleep Improvement Workbook

Made in the USA
Monee, IL
28 October 2024

68807484R00138